Using the Standards

Teacher Resource

Grade One

Published by Instructional Fair • TS Denison
an imprint of

Children's Publishing

Editors: Susan Fitzgerald, Rebecca Warren
Teacher Consultant: Lori De Goede

 **Children's Publishing**

Published by Instructional Fair • TS Denison
An imprint of McGraw-Hill Children's Publishing
Copyright © 2004 McGraw-Hill Children's Publishing

Send all inquiries to:
McGraw-Hill Children's Publishing
3195 Wilson Drive NW
Grand Rapids, Michigan 49544

Using the Standards: Teacher Resource—grade 1
ISBN: 0-7424-1941-X

1 2 3 4 5 6 7 8 9 PHXBK 09 08 07 06 05 04
The *McGraw-Hill* Companies

Table of Contents

Reading

Language Arts

Math

Science

Social Studies

Introduction

You can hardly spend a day in the world of education without hearing about standards. Teachers are asked to incorporate an increasingly complex array of state standards into an already crowded curriculum. But how do theoretical concepts translate into real-life student work? *Using the Standards* will help you fill your classroom with solid standards-based activities and answer your most pressing questions:

- How do I know what standards to follow?
- What grade-appropriate activities can I use with my students?
- How can I perform accurate and specific assessment of my students?
- What is the best way to prepare my students for standardized tests?

Developed with tested ideas from experienced teachers, this resource book is filled with ideas for making your classroom a dynamic, content-rich environment.

Finding "Your" Standards

Which standards should you follow? If your school has not specified which standards you are to follow, or if you are a home-based educator, a good place to start is your state standards. Most state standards can be found on a state's official web page under "education" **(www.statename.gov)**.

> **Hot Tip**
>
> **State Standards the Easy Way.** There is an easier way! Align to Achieve, Inc. has done the work for you. This not-for-profit organization has compiled state standards for every state into one easy-to-search database. You can find this database at: **www.aligntoachieve.org**.

National Standards?

Implementing standards-based education is not dependent on state models, however. Many agencies have issued so-called "national" standards. While an agreed-upon set of national standards does not, in fact, exist, there are nonetheless common themes throughout the different standard articulations. National standards are referenced in this book for each subject area only to provide a starting point for exploration into your own state or district standards. This book has been designed to cover a broad range of topics addressed by most standards. Give your students a solid foundation by working through the basic skills in this book, and you will find that every student can be far more than "up to standard."

How to Use This Book

Correlation to Standards

Begin with the "Correlation to Standards" chart on pages 10–12. After you have found your state standards (see page 4 for hints on how to do this), check the information for each content area to see which pages cover which skills. Blank spaces are available in the chart for you to record correlations to your own standards.

Parent Letter

As you begin to incorporate standards into your classroom, you may want to communicate this to parents. Use the "Parent Letter" on page 9 to let parents know what you are doing in the classroom and why. While most parents are aware that their children are required to take certain standardized tests, they often do not know that these tests are based on standards. The more involved the parents are in supporting your effort to include standards in the curriculum, the more likely your students will succeed.

Content Areas

See the individual content areas for more information about how to find standards-based material within that subject. Each subject area has its own distinctive icon to help you locate material quickly. This book contains the following content areas:

 Reading

 Language Arts

 Math

 Science

 Social Studies

For each of these subject areas, an information page explains the key features of standards in that subject. A clear summary of typical skills required by most standards for that area is followed by a list of classroom activities.

Activity Lists

You know the standards—now what? To help you translate theory into practice, we include an activity list for each subject area. Developed by experienced teachers who have used these activities in their classrooms, this list provides a great starting place for implementing the standards in your classroom. A variety of activities are included to appeal to different learning styles.

How To Use This Book

Sample Tests

Sample tests are included for each subject area. The tests are designed to give your students practice with the types of questions they may be asked on standardized tests. Use sample tests before beginning a new content area to identify skills that students need to practice, or use them after working through the activity pages to assess progress. See "Assessment Tips" on pages 7–8 for more ideas on measuring student achievement.

Skill Pages

Each content area includes skill-specific reproducible pages to use with your students. The pages included are not comprehensive, but do cover a broad range of expectations within each content area. Make as many copies as you need for your class and distribute to students. The skill pages can be done individually or in groups, in class as part of a center or at home. You may want to combine skill pages with ideas in the "Activity List" for each subject to help you develop your daily lesson plans.

Critical Thinking Themes

Look for the following themes on each page to help your students develop cross-curricular critical thinking skills:

- Explore
- Discover
- Organize
- Communicate
- Summarize

As students begin to explore the content of their world, discover new things, organize their thinking, communicate to others, and clearly summarize what they have learned, they will grow in their ability to analyze new information.

The value of standards-based learning is not simply to reach an end—performance on state tests—but for a beginning—allowing students to be full participants and investigators of the world around them.

Assessment Tips

All Students Can Succeed

One of the fundamental beliefs of a standards-based model for education is that all students can succeed. Rather than start with the assumption that a class will naturally include some students who will not succeed, teachers should start with the premise that all students can (and will) meet the standard. Students may differ in the ways they get there, but each should expect to achieve the same end result. The usefulness of the standards-based model is that it clearly and specifically states what that end result is to be. The challenge is to decide *how* to encourage learning that allows students at a wide range of skill levels to meet the standard and how to appropriately assess them along the way.

Assessment Requires Parent Involvement

Get parents involved early and often in the education of their child. Use the letter provided on page 9 to inform parents about the standards you will be covering and the tests (if any) that their child will be required to take. It is important to communicate to parents that one day of testing is nurtured by many days of involvement. Do what you can to keep parents up-to-date on the areas their child struggles with to encourage extra practice at home. As parents ask questions, review homework, and stay informed about learning goals, they will provide a sound platform for student success on standardized tests.

Assessment Is Ongoing

Whether aware of it or not, every teacher performs continuous assessment of students during class. How many times have you answered these questions during a class period?

- Which students offer answers quickly?
- Which students need more time to work through a problem?
- Who needs to use a hands-on tool to understand something?
- Who needs quiet time alone to work through a problem?
- Are there students who look frustrated? What do they need to understand?
- How can I adapt this lesson to encourage understanding?

Teachers naturally consider each student's progress as they move through a lesson. While it may be impossible to tailor learning for each member of a class, teachers should provide multiple opportunities for students to succeed. A variety of tools for solving problems will help students with different learning styles grasp essential concepts. This may include use of pictures, models, or other hands-on materials.

Instead of putting all the focus on the day of "the big test," create portfolios of a student's work throughout a unit. These can show progress in student thinking on a topic from the early days of learning to the end. They can also provide a flag for potential problem areas before testing occurs.

Assessment Tips

Assessment Is Varied

When designing tests, use a variety of formats. Depending on the age of your students, any of the following may be appropriate question types:

- true and false
- multiple choice
- matching
- fill-in-the-blank
- graphic organizers
- open-ended or essay

With younger students, you may also use one-on-one interviews to ask questions out loud and listen to students explain their answers.

Using a variety of types of assessment will allow students many different ways to show what they know. Encourage students to show the process by which they came to an answer; even if they did not achieve the correct end result, they may have a solid grasp on concepts. Showing all work will identify the specific place their solution process went awry.

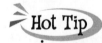

Begin with the End in Mind. Have you ever made it to the end of a great lesson series and found yourself stuck for ways to measure student progress? Rather than thinking of assessment as the end result, try beginning with the end in mind.

As you plan a new lesson series, consider what objectives you would like students to meet. Then ask yourself, how will I know if students have met those objectives? As you map out daily lesson plans, consider how each lesson will give students another tool to succeed on the testing they will face at the end of the unit.

Test Practice

For a complete practice in all content areas, see the McGraw-Hill Children's Publishing *Spectrum Test Practice* series. With a book for each grade level, this series provides a variety of practice questions and sample tests addressing the same standards used in this book.

Promoting the Standards
•encourage•remind•create•review•praise

Dear Parent/Guardian:

We have begun using activities in our classroom that are based on educational standards. "Standards" are guidelines for skills that students should know in a particular grade. Often standardized tests measure student achievement in these standard skills. By focusing our classroom activities on the standards, we are allowing the students to have as much practice as possible in these basic skills.

You can support your child's learning by understanding the standards that are required for his/her grade level. The standards that we are following can be found at

_____.

Your child will/will not be tested this year. The state test your child will take will be on _____. I am available at any time to review testing results and discuss how these scores affect your child's progress.

Encourage your child to rest well and eat a good breakfast before the test. You can help your child develop testing confidence by being involved in their learning throughout the school year.

To help your child do his/her best with this material, follow these guidelines:

- Encourage your child to be curious about the world.
- Remind your child to ask questions about things he/she does not understand in class.
- Create time for your child to share what he/she has discovered at school.
- Review the skill pages your child brings home. Ask which things your child had difficulty understanding.
- Praise your child often for learning. The end results on a single day of testing cannot measure enthusiasm, curiosity, or the joy of discovery.

With parents and teachers partnering together, we can be sure that our children are far more than "up to standard"!

Sincerely,

Correlation to Standards

Sample Standards

	Using the Standards Grade 1	*CAT Level for Gr. 1	**CTBS Level for Gr. 1	Other
Reading				
Word Analysis				
Recognizing letters				
Recognizing beginning, medial, and ending sounds	15, 16, 17, 21, 22, 23, 24	x	x	
Recognizing rhyming words	17, 25			
Recognizing compound words	15, 26			
Recognizing contractions	27			
Recognizing sight words	16, 29	x	x	
Vocabulary				
Using synonyms	30		x	
Using antonyms	31			
Matching pictures to words	18, 32, 35	x		
Categorizing words	33, 34	x	x	
Using context clues				
Understanding root words				
Reading Comprehension				
Identifying main idea with pictures	19, 42	x	x	
Identifying details	20, 37, 46, 47	x	x	
Matching pictures to sentences	41, 49	x	x	
Identifying sequence of events	36, 43, 48	x	x	
Making predictions		x	x	
Identifying character traits/feelings	15, 38, 39, 40, 45	x	x	
Distinguishing between reality and fantasy				
Identifying author's purpose	46, 47			
Reading various genre		x	x	
Language Arts				
Mechanics and Expression				
Using correct capitalization and punctuation	53, 57, 58, 59	x	x	
Determining correct usage	28, 52, 54, 60	x	x	
Recognizing sentences	51, 55, 61, 62	x	x	
Recognizing paragraphs	52, 56	x	x	
Spelling				
Identifying correct spelling	63	x	x	
Identifying incorrect spelling	51, 63	x	x	
Study Skills				
Using book parts				

*Terra Nova CAT™ ©2001 CTB/McGraw-Hill
**Terra Nova CTBS® ©1997 CTB/McGraw-Hill

Correlation to Standards

Grade 1

Sample Standards	Using the Standards Grade 1	*CAT Level for Gr. 1	**CTBS Level for Gr. 1	Other
Math				
Number and Operations				
Using number lines				
Using numbers up to 100			x	
Ordering and comparing whole numbers	72	x	x	
Using place value	74		x	
Recognizing fractions from pictures	76	x	x	
Demonstrating mastering of addition facts to 20	69, 77	x	x	
Solving two-digit addition and subtraction problems without regrouping	78, 79	x	x	
Other	73, 75	x	x	
Algebra		x	x	
Recognizing patterns with pictures	68, 81		x	
Extending number patterns		x	x	
Using number sentences				
Using symbols to represent numbers	68, 83			
Probability				
Collecting data	85, 98	x	x	
Interpreting data	86, 99		x	
Geometry				
Identifying shapes	70, 88, 89		x	
Identifying line of symmetry			x	
Identifying congruent figures	90	x	x	
Measurement				
Using standard and non-standard measures	91, 92, 93	x	x	
Selecting appropriate measures				
Estimating				
Measuring to the nearest inch	94	x	x	
Reading thermometers	95			
Telling time to the half hour	96	x	x	
Recognizing coins	97	x	x	
Problem Solving				
Selecting appropriate operations	77, 82		x	
Using a variety of methods to solve problems, including graphs, tables, and charts	86, 87, 98, 99	x	x	

*Terra Nova CAT™ ©2001 CTB/McGraw-Hill
**Terra Nova CTBS® ©1997 CTB/McGraw-Hill

Grade 1

Sample Standards

	Using the Standards Grade 1	*CAT Level for Gr. 1	**CTBS Level for Gr. 1	Other
Science				
Science				
Understanding plant and animal attributes	103, 104, 108, 109	x	x	
Understanding properties of materials	105	x	x	
Understanding the water cycle	106	x		
Understanding the types of matter	103, 107	x	x	
Environment	102			
Seasons	102			
Social Studies				
Social Studies				
Comparing the past and present in their community	119	x	x	
Identifying rights and responsibilities	114, 115			
Explaining the difference between maps and globes	113, 117, 118	x	x	
Locating community on U.S. maps	120, 121, 122	x	x	
Identifying the basic vocabulary of economics	116	x	x	
Other	112			

*Terra Nova CAT™   ©2001 CTB/McGraw-Hill
**Terra Nova CTBS®   ©1997 CTB/McGraw-Hill

Standards in Reading

Reading provides the framework on which all other content areas rest. Developing good reading skills will serve students well as they continue to explore ideas in science, mathematics, social studies, or the arts. National initiatives focused on reading point to the importance of reading for future academic and personal achievement. The National Council of Teachers of English (NCTE) standards can be found at: **www.ncte.org/standards**. To be sure your students' reading skills lay the foundation for future success, consider the building blocks of reading: vocabulary and comprehension.

Word Analysis

Word analysis provides a clear understanding of letters and words. It shows how they look, their names, and how they are related to specific sounds. Students learn that words are made up of a sequence of sounds, identify some sounds in words, and connect them to letters. Standards-based reading activities will give students grade-appropriate practice with:

- Letter Recognition
- Letter Sounds
- Rhyming Words
- Sight Words
- Compound Words
- Contractions

Vocabulary

Vocabulary development begins in the very earliest grades as students learn to recognize words and understand their meanings. Standards-based reading activities will give students grade-appropriate practice with:

- Synonyms, Antonyms, Homonyms
- Multiple-Meaning Words
- Rhyming and Rhythmic language

Encourage your students to use a variety of strategies to decode the meaning of unknown words—using a dictionary or thesaurus, using context clues, or looking for common root words. Your students should encounter words in many different ways—from looking at individual words on vocabulary lists, to listening to words read out loud as part of a story. Developing fluency with language means being able to understand words as they are spoken, heard, and written. As students become more adept at working with individual words, they will be able to turn their focus to comprehension and interpretation of what they have read.

Standards in Reading

Comprehension

Students of all ages should practice reading a variety of texts, from poetry to stories, from information books to science reports. Create a text-rich classroom by establishing theme-based centers with appropriate reading material. Students need multiple ways to approach reading, so include a place for listening to stories and a place for writing and responding to what others have written.

Everyone Loves a Story. Students of all ages love stories. To help students develop fluency in reading, plan a regular story time. Go around the room and have students each take a turn reading out loud. This encourages students to develop fluency, listening skills, and comprehension—all while enjoying the what-happens-next excitement that only stories can bring!

Students demonstrate comprehension of what they have read through their ability to identify the following:

- Main Idea with Pictures
- Details
- Sequence of Events
- Making Predictions, Drawing Conclusions
- Distinguishing between Reality and Fantasy
- Author's Purpose
- Character Traits/Feelings
- Type of Writing (Genre)

These skills will vary by grade level, but all have the same purpose—understanding what has been read. A variety of activities can help students focus on and interpret what they have read.

- Have your students work with graphic organizers to help them identify key ideas and connections among them.
- Create text-based questions that have students either recollect what they have read or develop strategies for skimming through the text to find an answer.
- Allow your students to create questions of their own or draw a picture in response to what they have read.
- Encourage students to make connections between what they have read and their own life experiences.

As students develop vocabulary and comprehension, they will read with greater fluency and understanding. The foundation set by these basic skills in reading will prove to be strong and solid for the years of learning that are to come.

Activity List

Activity 1–Sound Match-Up

- **Standards:** Beginning and ending sounds
- **Goal:** Students will use word cards to find matching beginning or ending sounds.
- **Materials:** You will need clip art from a computer or clip art book, crayons or colored pencils, scissors, glue or paste, and index cards to laminate.
- **Activity:** Make your own word cards with clip art from a computer or clip art book. Color pictures, cut them out, and laminate on index cards. Have the students play games to find matching beginning or ending sounds on two cards. They can keep the cards when they find a match and the one with the most cards at the end wins the game.

Activity 2–Compound Word Game

- **Standard:** Compound words
- **Goal:** Students will learn to make a compound word by combining two nouns on word cards.
- **Materials:** You will need pencils and index cards.
- **Activity:** Make cards with nouns that could make a compound word. Turn cards upside down and spread on a flat surface. Have students randomly pick two cards. If the two chosen cards make a real compound word, they keep the cards. If the words do not make a compound word, they return the cards where they found them.
- **Extension:** Give each student a compound word to break the word into two separate words. Next, the students illustrate each individual word and then illustrate the compound word as a whole.

Activity 3–"Who Am I?"

- **Standard:** Identifying character traits
- **Goal:** Students will identify a character in a story from the character traits you give them or they can make a list of character traits of a character you assign them.
- **Materials:** You will need a story to read to the class, such as a fairy tale with lots of characters. Also, the students will need paper and pencils to make a list.
- **Activity:** Read a story to the class. Then, read a list of character traits to the students and have them guess which character you are describing from the story. You can also have the students do this by assigning them a character and have them list the character traits, and then read them to the class. This works really well with a fairy tale with lots of characters.

Once upon a time...

Activity List

Activity 4–Picture This

- **Standard:** Recognizing letters
- **Goal:** Students will learn to recognize letters by bringing items from home that begin with their letter.
- **Materials:** You will need poster boards, scissors, and space to display items brought from home. Also, if you wish to take pictures of the students with their letters and matching items, you'll need a digital camera, regular camera, or a video camera. You could also put the pictures in a scrapbook.
- **Activity:** Assign each student a letter. Ask them to bring in items from home that begin with their letter. Have them make a big cut-out of their letter out of poster board. Using a digital camera, regular camera, or video camera, take pictures of the students with their cut-out letter and items that begin with that letter. Make a class book out of the pictures or show the whole video to the class to discover what their classmates found.

Activity 5–POP! Game

- **Standard:** Sight words
- **Goal:** Students will learn to recognize sight words using sight word cards.
- **Materials:** You will need index cards to laminate, scissors, and pencils.
- **Activity:** This game can be called whatever you wish, based on the die-cuts you choose for the word cards. For POP!, make sight word cards in the shape of balloons or ovals, and then laminate the cards. You will also need to make four or five cards with POP! on them. To play, you show each student a card, one at a time. If the student can read the word on the first chance, they get to keep the card and then you move to the next student. If a student gets a POP! card, they need to give you their stack of cards. Play for the allotted time and then have the students count their cards. The player with the most cards wins the game.

Activity 6–Story Puzzles

- **Standard:** Identifying sequence of events
- **Goal:** Students will learn to identify the sequence of events in stories.
- **Materials:** You will need paper for sentence strips and a marker to write on them.
- **Activity:** Write sentences from a story on sentence strips and have the students work as teams to put the story back together from beginning to end.

Name _____ Date _____

Sample Test: Word Analysis

➤ **Listen as your teacher reads the question and says the name of the picture. Then listen as your teacher reads the word choices. Circle the best answer. Examples 1 and 2 are done for you.**

| Examples |

1. What word has the same vowel sound as the picture?

   (a.) pear
   b. spoon
   c. kite
   d. chip

2. What word rhymes with car?

   a. ball
   b. cat
   c. bat
   (d.) star

3. What word has the same vowel sound as the picture?

   a. mouse
   b. long
   c. tick
   d. moon

5. What word has the same vowel sound as kite?

   a. pin
   b. time
   c. from
   d. soul

4. What word has the same vowel sound as the picture?

   a. bead
   b. hive
   c. quilt
   d. apple

6. What word rhymes with cat?

   a. crow
   b. pool
   c. sat
   d. snake

STOP

Name _____ Date _____

Sample Test: Vocabulary

▶ **Look at the pictures. Listen as your teacher reads the word choices. Circle the letter of the word that goes with each picture. Examples 1 and 2 are done for you.**

Examples

1. **a.** cap
    b. box
    c. ball ⟵circled

2. **a.** kick
    b. throw ⟵circled
    c. stand

3. **a.** dance
    b. run
    c. swing

4. **a.** tire
    b. slide
    c. bird

7. **a.** sled
    b. car
    c. boat

8. **a.** cat
    b. fish
    c. turtle

5. **a.** skating
    b. camping
    c. shopping

6. **a.** tent
    b. house
    c. truck

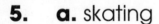

9. **a.** baseball
    b. soccer
    c. tennis

10. **a.** singing
    b. walking
    c. catching

STOP

0-7424-1941-X — *Using the Standards*

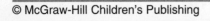

Name _____ Date _____

Sample Test: Comprehension

Listen to your teacher read the sentences. Match a picture to the sentences. Example 1 is done for you. Circle the letter of the picture that goes with each sentence.

Example

1. This floats high in the sky. People like to ride in them.

a.

(b.)

c.

2. It was very cold. Mom said to wear these.

a.

b.

c.

3. We were late. We had to get there fast.

a.

b.

c.

4. A boy is _____.

  a. whispering

  b. jumping

  c. eating

5. The other boy is _____.

  a. talking

  b. listening

  c. sleeping

STOP

0-7424-1941-X — Using the Standards

Sample Test: Comprehension

➡ **Listen to your teacher read the story and the questions. Circle the letter of the best answer for each question.**

Ahoy!

A ship is a very large boat. Some ships can cross the whole ocean. Ships carry people and cargo from one place to another. People who run a ship are called sailors. Sailors use the word *ahoy* to hail a ship.

A ship has many parts. The stern is the back of the ship and the bow is the front. The ship's steering wheel is called the helm. You can turn the ship right or left with the helm.

Some ships have sails, which are attached to masts. The sails are like big sheets. They catch the wind and help ships go fast. There could also be a crow's nest high up on the mast. A sailor

I. What is a ship?

   a. a train

   b. a very large boat

   c. a raft

2. Where do many ships travel?

   a. across the ocean

   b. in rivers

   c. in ponds

3. What do sails do?

   a. carry people

   b. cover people

   c. help the ship go

4. Why did the author write this story?

   a. to tell about sailors

   b. to tell about ships

   c. so people would buy ships

STOP

Name _____ Date _____

Name That Picture

▶ **Say the name of each picture. Circle the letter that you hear at the beginning. Then write the letter on the line.**

1.
_____
------- s
_____ t

2.
_____
------- d
_____ c

3.
_____
------- s
_____ g

4.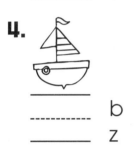
_____
------- b
_____ z

5.
_____
------- t
_____ p

6.
_____
------- m
_____ b

7.
_____
------- j
_____ g

8.
_____
------- r
_____ l

9.
_____
------- l
_____ c

▶ **Say the name of each picture. Then write the letter that makes the beginning sound.**

10.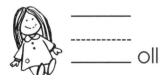
_____

_____ oll

11.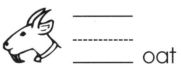
_____

_____ oat

12.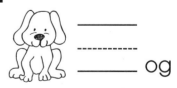
_____

_____ og

13.
_____

_____ ipper

14.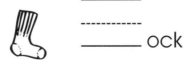
_____

_____ ock

15.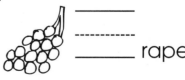
_____

_____ rape

0-7424-1941-X — Using the Standards

Snack Pack

⮞ **Say the name of each picture. Circle the letter that makes the ending sound. Then write the letter on the line.**

1.

_____
------- f
_____ g

2.

_____
------- t
_____ c

3.

_____
------- p
_____ r

4.

_____
------- k
_____ b

5.

_____
------- x
_____ b

6.

_____
------- p
_____ m

7.

_____
------- t
_____ f

8.

_____
------- h
_____ t

⮞ **Say the name of each picture. Then write the letter that makes the ending sound.**

9.

ba _____

10.

pi _____

11.

be _____

12.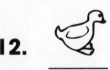

duc _____

13.

pe _____

14.

si _____

0-7424-1941-X — *Using the Standards*

Name _____ Date _____

Which Whale?

▶ **Read each sentence. Use the wh words in the Word Box to write the missing words on the lines.**

Word Box

which	when
whale	what
where	wheel

1. _____ are we going after school?

2. _____ movie should we see?

3. A huge _____ swam near the ship.

4. _____ are we going to the Children's Museum?

5. The shopping cart has a broken _____ .

Let It Snow

➡ **Use the r blend words in the Word Box to write the missing words on the lines.**

Word Box
grow   treat
friend   cream

_____

1. My _____ and I like winter.

_____

2. Greg likes whipped _____ on his hot cocoa.

_____

3. You should always _____ others kindly.

_____

4. The seeds I planted are starting to _____ .

➡ **Match each group of letters to an l blend. Write the words on the lines.**

ant   ag   ug   ake

pl   **fl**

_____   _____

_____   _____

_____   _____

_____   _____

Name _____ Date _____

What to Do at the Zoo?

➤ **Write the words from the Word Box that rhyme with each animal's name.**

```
············································
·              Word Box                    ·
·   bake     meal     wake     wear        ·
·   feel     too      care     you         ·
············································
```

snake

_____   _____

bear

_____   _____

kangaroo

_____   _____

seal

_____   _____

0-7424-1941-X — *Using the Standards*

Compound Kittens

➡ **If the two words on a kitten make a compound word, write them together on a line. Put an X on the kitten if the words do not make a compound word. Color the kittens that do not have an X.**

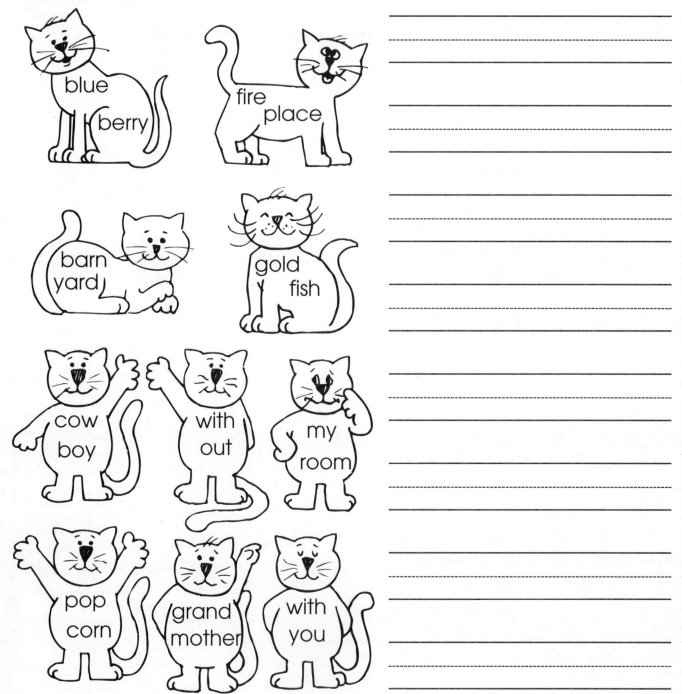

Name _____ Date _____

We're Happy!

 A **contraction** is a short way of writing two words. We use an apostrophe in a contraction to show that a letter or letters have been left out.
Example: I'm = I am

➡ **Draw a line from each pair of words to the right contraction.**

he is •   • it's

it is •   • she's

she is •   • he's

they are •   • you're

you are •   • they're

0-7424-1941-X — Using the Standards

Name _____   Date _____

Chirp, Chirp

Some words tell about sounds and about actions that go with sounds.

Example: dog—bark
bee—buzz

➡ **Find a word from the Word Box that describes each picture. Write the word under the picture.**

> **Word Box**
> chirp   crash   boom
> pop   bang   gulp

Name _____ Date _____

My Backyard

1.

2.

► **Cut and paste...**
- the dog **between** the tree and the bush.
- the kite **next** to the tree.
- the cat in **front** of the tree.
- the ball **beside** the doghouse.
- the sun **up** in the sky.

3.

4.

5.

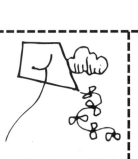

0-7424-1941-X — *Using the Standards*

Circus Fun

➡ **Synonyms are words that mean nearly the same thing. If the underlined words in each pair of sentences are synonyms, color the circle yellow. If they are not, color the circle red.**

◯ Maxine laughed at the silly clowns.
Ally giggled, too.

◯ The acrobats were high above them.
There was no net below.

◯ The two friends watched the acrobats.
They stared in wonder.

◯ Ally clapped for the elephants.
Maxine watched them parade around the ring.

◯ Next came the pretty horses.
The white one was the most beautiful.

◯ The girls always loved the circus.
They wished they could stay forever.

Name _____   Date _____

Growing Up

➤ **Antonyms are words that mean the opposite. Circle the word in the second sentence that is the opposite of the underlined word in the first sentence. Color the picture that tells about the second sentence.**

1.	My plant is little. If I put it near a sunny window, it will be big some day.	
2.	Joey's soup is too cold. He would like some hot soup.	
3.	Mallory's boots are old. She needs new ones.	
4.	The kitten can't get down. Dad will go up to get it.	
5.	I have work to do. Then I can play a game with you.	

     0-7424-1941-X — *Using the Standards*

A Day at the Park

➡️ **Some words sound the same even though they are spelled differently and have different meanings. Color the picture that shows the meaning of the underlined word.**

1.	Sergio's family went to the park.	
2.	His brother fished from the bank.	
3.	His sister fed a duck some bread crumbs.	
4.	It was fun to watch her.	
5.	Then Mom got the picnic basket from the trunk.	

Owls Hoot

➡ **Nouns are words that name people, places, or things. Verbs are action words. Write the words where they belong.**

Word Box

play	children	sun	bedroom
barks	dog	hop	shines
rabbits	sleep	lunch	eat

Nouns	**Verbs**
_____	_____
_____	_____
_____	_____
_____	_____
_____	_____
_____	_____
_____	_____
_____	_____
_____	_____
_____	_____

How Are You?

Use **is** and **are** to tell about now.
Use **is** to tell about one person or thing.
Use **are** to tell about more than one.
Use **are** with the word **you**.
Use **am** with the word **I**.

➤ **Write is, are, or am in each sentence below.**

1. The lake _____ deep.

2. I _____ fishing.

3. Marta _____ baiting a hook.

4. Amar and Tommy _____ coming to our cabin.

5. I _____ going to cook the fish for dinner.

6. You _____ invited, too.

0-7424-1941-X — *Using the Standards*

Tyrone Turtle

**Match the story titles with the pictures below.
Write the letters on the lines.**

a. Tyrone Finds His Home **d.** Tyrone Learns to Read
b. Tyrone Dives In **e.** Tyrone Slides in the Snow
c. Tyrone Makes Dinner **f.** Tyrone Takes a Nap

1. _____

2. _____

3. _____

4. _____

5. _____

6. _____

For Fun! Choose one of the titles above and write a story about Tyrone Turtle.

The Big Top

➡️ **A sentence has a beginning and an ending. Draw a line to match the beginning and ending of each sentence. Write the number in the box by each picture.**

1. A big flag   has two balloons.

2. The little boy   likes to eat peanuts.

3. The circus clown   is holding cotton candy.

4. The elephant   is on the circus tent.

5. The woman   is wearing funny shoes.

0-7424-1941-X — *Using the Standards*

Sky Blue

➤ **A sentence needs special words. Look at each picture. Write two words that tell something about the picture. Use the words in a sentence about the picture.**

_____

- -

_____

- -

_____

- -

The Lion and the Mouse

▶ **Read the story. Answer the questions on page 39.**

After eating a big meal, a lion took a nap. Something ran across his back and woke him up. He stretched out his big paw. He caught a little mouse.

The mouse squeaked, "I am too small to be a good meal for you. Please let me go!"

"No!" roared the lion.

"Let me go. Someday I may be able to help you," the little mouse cried.

The lion laughed. "What could a tiny mouse do for a mighty lion?" But, since he was not hungry, he let the mouse go.

The next day, the mouse heard a roar for help.

Hunters had trapped the lion in a big net. The little mouse ran to the lion. She chewed the net with her sharp teeth. She chewed and chewed until the lion was free!

"Thank you," said the lion.

The lion and the mouse became good friends.

The Lion and the Mouse (cont.)

▶ **Circle the right answers about *The Lion and the Mouse* on page 38.**

1. The characters are _____.

    kids   animals   fish

2. The characters are _____.

    real   make-believe

3. Which character said "Please let me go!"?

    lion   mouse

4. Which character said "What could a mouse do for me?"

    lion   mouse

5. Why did the lion let the little mouse go?

    He was kind.   He was not hungry.

6. Why did the mouse chew the lion's net?

    She was afraid.   She said she would help him.

▶ **Write words from the Word Box that tell about each character on the line under its name.**

Word Box

big   small   sharp teeth

roars   squeaks   big paws

Lion _____

_____

_____

Mouse _____

_____

_____

 0-7424-1941-X — Using the Standards

Soft Woolly Lamb

Describing words tell about a person, place, or thing. They can tell how things look, taste, sound, or feel.

➡ **Find and circle the two describing words in each sentence.**

1. The white kitten is fluffy.

2. Two noisy squirrels ran up a tree.

3. This old book is torn.

4. The apple was sweet and crisp.

5. The bright sun is warm on my neck.

6. Six ducks swam in a round pond.

Uh-Oh!

Write the letters on the lines to match each story to its picture.

1. Pedro got his puppy's leash and walked into the backyard. Then he mumbled, "Uh-oh!" _____

2. Pedro put on his boots, coat, mittens, and hat. He got his sled and walked to the top of the hill. He looked down the hill. "Uh-oh," he moaned. _____

3. Scout was very hungry. He had played ball with Pedro all morning. He ran to his food bowl. "Uh-oh," whined the puppy.

_____

4. Mom planned to cook eggs for breakfast. She set the carton of eggs on the table. Scout jumped up and pulled on the tablecloth. Mom said, "Uh-oh." _____

Name _____ Date _____

Camping Trip

➡️ **A sentence tells a whole idea. Look at the picture. Write four sentences that tell about something in the picture.**

_____

_____

_____

_____

_____

_____

_____

_____

Name _____ Date _____

Doghouse Duties

➡ **The words in a sentence must be in the correct order. Write 1-4 in the circles to put the words in order. Write each sentence correctly on the line.**

A. 

painting.   doghouse   needs   Ralph's

_____

- -

B.

have   I   paint.   red

_____

- -

C.

brushes.   two   here   are

_____

- -

D.

happy.   very   is   Ralph

_____

- -

What Do You Think?

▶ **Read each story. Circle the correct answer.**

Arnold has been riding his bicycle after school for two years. He is tired of riding his bicycle every day. He wants to do something new. Arnold's friend asks him if he wants to swim at the YMCA after school.

1. What will Arnold do?
   a. Arnold will swim.
   b. Arnold will ride his bicycle.

Rena loves her uncle. He is very special to her. Rena wants to buy a birthday present for her uncle. He likes fishing. She wants to buy him a book about fishing but she doesn't have enough money. Rena saves her money for two months. Finally, she has enough money for the book.

2. What will Rena do?
   a. Rena will buy herself a new video game.
   b. Rena will buy a book about fishing for her uncle.

How Are You Feeling?

➤ **Read each sentence. Write the name of the character on the line after the sentence that shows how he or she feels.**

Carina Dermot Johann Bridget Lian

1. "I was so angry, I broke my pencil!" yelled _____.

2. "I was afraid when our lights went out last night," said _____.

3. "Mom and Dad said I could have a birthday party," said _____.

4. "I can't play outside today because it's raining. I am bored," said _____.

5. "I fell off my bike and hurt my knee," said _____.

6. "The thunder and lightning scared me!" cried _____.

7. "We are going to the beach today," said _____.

8. "Someone cut in front of me in line!" said_____.

Name _____ Date _____

You Can Make a Difference

▶ **Read the paragraphs below and answer the questions on page 47.**

Air pollution causes many problems. It makes air unsafe to breathe and makes some people sick. Smoke causes air pollution. Smoke can carry dangerous chemicals in the air. Cars also cause air pollution. Cutting down too many trees is bad for the air.

What can people do to help stop air pollution and make the air safer? People can plant more trees. Trees take away polluted air and make the air fresh. People can find a safer way to burn fuel. People can also drive their cars less. People can make a difference.

You Can Make a Difference

➤ **Answer the questions below about the story on page 46.**

1. What does air pollution do to the air?

_____

_____

2. Write two things that cause air pollution.

_____

_____

3. Write three ways people can help stop air pollution.

_____

_____

_____

_____

_____

_____

4. Why do you think the author wrote this?

_____

_____

_____

_____

_____

Important Lessons

➡ **Read the beginning and middle of each story.
Write your own ending.**

1. Mr. Hare and Mr. Tortoise lined up for the
start of the race. Mr. Hare ran very fast.
He was far ahead of Mr. Tortoise. Mr.
Hare laid down under a tree to take a nap.

What happened next?

_____

_____

_____

_____

_____

_____

2. A crow stole a piece of cheese from a picnic. She flew up
in a tree to eat it. A hungry fox saw the crow. He wanted
her cheese. He called to the crow, "Oh, pretty
crow! Your feathers are so shiny. If your voice is
sweet too, then you must be a queen." The silly
crow was tricked by the fox. She started to sing.

What happened next?

_____

_____

_____

_____

_____

Name _____ Date _____

True Stories?

There are different kinds of stories. Some are true and some are make-believe. The **setting** of a story could be a real place or a place you made up.

➤ **Read each paragraph. Write one of the settings below on the line.**

> outer space   forest

1. Lester was hungry. He ran down the tree trunk. He pawed at the dead leaves. He wanted the nut he had hid yesterday. He dug and dug. It wasn't there! He looked at all the other trees. Now, where did he hide that nut?

_____

2. Jamie looked out the window. He could see Earth behind him. It looked very small from way out here. Then he looked at Pluto. That's where he was headed. He hope he would like his new home.

_____

➤ **In which setting above do you think a real story could have taken place? Make-believe stories can take place in real settings, too.**

Standards in Language Arts

Along with developing reading skills comes the understanding that language is indeed an art. The National Council of Teachers of English (NCTE) standards for language arts can be found at: **www.ncte.org/standards**. From the earliest writings of the young student to the more sophisticated arguments of the older student, progress in language arts is measured in terms of mechanics and expression.

Mechanics and Expression

A standards-based language arts curriculum will refine writing skills in students as they create their own works and evaluate the works of others. Students should have a solid grasp of the following language conventions:

- Capitalization and Punctuation
- Spelling
- Sentence Structure
- Grammar and Usage

Students should repeatedly practice the steps of the writing process—prewriting, draft, editing/revising, and publishing. Collect portfolios of a student's work from prewriting to publishing so students have a firm grasp not only of the effort involved in creative writing, but also the joys of the end result. A published collection of class projects is a wonderful way to share the work of your students with parents and schoolmates.

> **Copycat Writing.** Let your students learn from the best writers around. As part of your reading time, have students pick out their favorite part of a story. Choose a sentence or two to look at as a class. Write them on the board. Talk about why that sentence is effective and what techniques the author used. Then encourage your students to be copycats. Can they write a sentence of their own using the author's as a model? Make a "copycat corner" in your room, displaying the author's original sentence along with your students' versions.

As students learn the techniques that go into the craft of putting words together, they will begin to see language as an art and seek out that art in their own reading and writing.

Activity List

Activity 1–Help the Teacher!

- **Standard:** Spelling
- **Goal:** Students will learn to identify incorrect spelling and correct it.
- **Materials:** You will need paper and pencils.
- **Activity:** The teacher writes a morning message to the students with spelling errors. The students need to rewrite the message finding the mistakes that the teacher made. When the students are finished, they help the teacher correct the mistakes.

Activity 2–Silly Sentences

- **Standard:** Recognizing sentences
- **Goal:** Students will learn to recognize sentences by picking word cards with a noun, an adjective, a verb, and another noun to make up a sentence.
- **Materials:** You will need index cards and a marker.
- **Activity:** Brainstorm nouns, adjectives, and verbs as a class. Write the different words on index cards. Have the students take turns picking an adjective, a noun, a verb, and another noun. The students need to make a silly sentence out of the words and then illustrate the sentence.

Activity 3–Missing Words

- **Standard:** Recognizing sentences
- **Goal:** Students will learn to create a sentence by using context clues to figure out what word is missing.
- **Materials:** You will need paper to make sentence strips, a marker, and sticky notes.
- **Activity:** Write sentences from a current story or poem on sentence strips. Use sticky notes to cover up words from the sentences. Have the students use context clues to figure out what word is missing.

Activity 4–Sentences Under Construction

- **Standard:** Recognizing sentences
- **Goal:** Students will learn to construct sentences by putting words together from sentences that have been cut into pieces.
- **Materials:** You will need paper for sentence strips and for the students to write on, and a marker and pencils for the students.
- **Activity:** Write sentences on sentence strips and cut into pieces. The students need to put the sentences together so they make sense. Then have the students write the sentences they make on paper.

 Activity 5–Paragraphs Under Construction ....

- **Standard:** Recognizing paragraphs
- **Goal:** Students will learn to recognize a paragraph by putting sentences from a paragraph back together in the correct order.
- **Materials:** You will need paper for sentence strips and for the students to write on, and a marker and pencils for the students.
- **Activity:** Write sentences from a current story or nonfiction book on sentence strips. Number the sentence strips on the back in the correct order of how they are in the paragraph to allow students to check their work. Have students put the paragraph back together as a class or individually.

 Activity 6–Simply Superlative ....

- **Standard:** Determining correct usage
- **Goal:** Students will identify which superlative adjectives for each situation.
- **Materials:** You will need collections of 3 similar objects for comparison and adjectives to describe them written in large letters on cards. (Example: 3 balls of different sizes and cards saying "small, smaller, smallest.")
- **Activity:** A fun way to help students understand the correct form of adjective to use is by using objects. You can begin by calling 3 students of different heights to the front of the room and arranging them by height. Give the students cards saying "tall, taller, tallest" and ask them to choose the correct card. Have the class give a "thumbs up" if each student has the correct adjective. You can repeat this activity with a variety of objects and call 3 students up each time to select the appropriate adjective.

 Activity 7–Stop and Go Usage ....

- **Standard:** Determining correct usage
- **Goal:** Students will identify sentences with correct usage by holding up a "Stop" or "Go" sign.
- **Materials:** You will need several pairs of sentences, some with usage errors, some without, and two reproducible pages—one with a "Stop" sign, one with a "Go" traffic light.
- **Activity:** Have students color the "Go" green on their traffic light and the "Stop" red. Then tell them you will be reading sentences out loud to them, some with errors in them. If the sentence sounds correct, they should hold up their "Go" sign. If it does not sound correct, they should hold up their "Stop" sign. If students hold up the "Stop" sign, see if they can figure out what needs to be changed in each sentence.

Sample Test: Sentences

Listen to your teacher read these groups of words. Circle the letter of the group that makes a complete sentence. Examples 1 and 2 are done for you.

Examples

1. a. To the store.

(b.) The tree house is high up in the tree.

c. Won the race.

2. a. The butterfly.

(b.) The sun rose.

c. Moon shining.

---

3. a. Our yard.

b. It rained all night.

c. Thunder loud.

6. a. When was the?

b. Was open all day.

c. The pizza was good.

---

4. a. Maggie saw the moon.

b. In the sky.

c. Some people.

7. a. See the.

b. Is cold.

c. It snows in the winter.

---

5. a. Black cat is.

b. Bird nests.

c. Fred has a new coat.

8. a. We like popcorn.

b. Likes to sing.

c. Rabbit in hat.

STOP

Sample Test: Paragraphs

➤ **A paragraph is a group of sentences that are about the same idea. Listen to your teacher read the groups of sentences and the answer choices. Circle the sentence that best completes the paragraph. Example I is done for you.**

Examples

I. It rained hard. There were many mud puddles. _____

a. Birds built nests.

b. We splashed in the water.

c. The sun was hot.

➤ **Circle the correct sentence that finishes each paragraph.**

2. Gino sat down to read. He read a long time. _____

a. He finished the book.

b. It was his favorite toy.

c. The TV was loud.

3. The family went on a trip. They were going far away. _____

a. They went on skates.

b. They took an airplane.

c. Sandi did not like the pickle.

4. It was a nice day. I looked up at the sky. _____

a. I ate a cookie.

b. I saw fluffy clouds.

c. The grass was prickly.

5. Andrea is my sister. She is older than I am. _____

a. My dog is funny.

b. She is also taller than I am.

c. Our cat purrs.

➤ **A sentence begins with a capital letter and ends with a period. Read the words that go with each picture. Draw a line between the words to make two sentences. Write each sentence correctly on the lines. Number one has been started for you.**

1. i have a new bike / it is blue

_____
_____
_____
_____

2. we are selling fruit we have a fruit stand

_____
_____
_____
_____

3. i have a new dog i got him at the Pet Shop

_____
_____
_____
_____

4. i love my doll her name is Marcie

_____
_____
_____
_____

Where's My Cave?

➤ **A telling sentence ends with a period. An asking sentence ends with a question mark. Read each sentence. Put the correct mark in each box.**

1. It is snowing in the forest ☐

2. Why isn't the bear sleeping through the winter ☐

3. The trees are covered with snow ☐

4. Which tree is the smallest ☐

5. The bear is looking for his cave ☐

6. It is almost time for Christmas ☐

Name _____ Date _____

Summer Vacation

➡ **An asking sentence begins with a capital letter and ends with a question mark. Write each question correctly on the lines.**

1. how was your vacation

_____

- -

_____

2. where did you go

_____

- -

_____

3. did you ride in a train or a car

_____

- -

_____

4. how long was your trip

_____

- -

_____

5. did you take pictures

_____

- -

_____

By the Sea

 Words that sound the same may not mean the same or be spelled the same.

Example: I **know** how to read.
I have **no** time to watch TV today.

▶ **Read the sentences below. Write the correct words that go with the pictures on the lines.**

1. George _____ a cookie.

ate
eight

2. Sara has _____ pencils.

to
two

3. The _____ is bumpy.

rode
road

4. _____ can ride a bike.

eye
I

5. What do you _____ in the picture?

see
sea

Fish Swim

▶ **Match the nouns and verbs to make complete sentences. Write the sentences next to the matching pictures.**

Nouns
The stars
An airplane
The top
The baby
A duck

Verbs
smiled.
shine.
flies.
quacks.
spins.

1. _____
_____

2. _____
_____

3. _____
_____

4. _____
_____

5. _____
_____

Making Sense

➡ **A sentence must make sense. Read the beginning of each sentence. Circle the correct ending. Write another ending for the sentence on the line.**

1. My mom

likes her job.

is going to summer camp with me.

_____

_____

2. Two sheep

until it rains again.

ran down the hill.

_____

_____

3.  Our school

behind the brick wall.

had a bake sale.

_____

_____

4. Toshi

bought some candy.

fell asleep.

_____

_____

5.  My class

sat until three o'clock.

went to the Art Museum.

_____

_____

 0-7424-1941-X — *Using the Standards*

Honey Bee

➤ **Circle the misspelled words. Then write the correct words from the Word Box on the lines.**

```
................................................
·         Word Box                              ·
·   free     prize     drive     frog           ·
·   cross    grass     train     grade          ·
................................................
```

I. Look both ways before you kros the street.   _____

2. My sister is in the third graid.   _____

3. A ladybug landed on a blade of graz.   _____

4. We won a fee pass to the movies.   _____

5. A tiny froj hopped into the pond.   _____

6. They rode the little chrain at the carnival.   _____

7. I won the grand prise at the spelling bee.   _____

8. His mother will dive them to school.   _____

Standards in Math

Standards-based math activities encourage students to explore mathematical processes in different contexts. To begin to implement math standards in your class, a great starting place is the standard framework developed by the National Council of Teachers of Mathematics (NCTM). For more on the NCTM standards, see: **standards.nctm.org**. NCTM divides mathematical standards into the following content strands:

- Number and Operations
- (Pre-) Algebra
- Geometry
- Measurement
- Problem Solving
- Data Analysis and Probability

The NCTM process strands—Problem Solving, Reasoning and Proof, Connections, Communication, and Representation—describe the different ways that students come to understand and apply mathematical knowledge. Developing a standards-based mathematical curriculum is as much about how you teach as what you teach. The process strands provide a solid base for understanding how to work through content learning.

Problem Solving

Recognizing that students use a variety of processes to get to a solution, teachers should encourage discussion by asking frequently: "How did you get that answer? What steps did you take?" As students communicate their ideas to others, they better understand the processes they are using and find new tools for problem solving in the strategies of others.

Students should have practice solving problems in a variety of contexts—from math equations to story problems about real-life situations. This develops critical thinking skills and provides an answer to that ever-popular question: "When will I use this?"

Reasoning and Proof

Once students have come to an answer, they should spend a moment reflecting: "Does the answer make sense? What tools can be used to prove the answer?" Reasoning and proof will vary depending on the level of your students, but there are some basic principles to use for all math situations. Students can draw a picture or use an opposite operation to help them understand—not only if an answer is true, but also why.

Standards in Math

Communication

Students can learn as much from each other as from the teacher when given the chance to organize and explain their work. Seeing how someone else solved a problem may unlock the key of understanding for a student who has been stuck using a different strategy. Encourage students to communicate using their own words, symbols, and mathematical vocabulary. Spend time talking—not just about the answer, but the various ways to get there.

Connections

As students gain mathematical knowledge, it is important to make connections between different branches of mathematics. For example, an understanding of the number system and place value provides the foundation for developing skills in algebra or geometry. Relating mathematics to real-world situations with which students are familiar significantly improves retention and problem-solving abilities. Students develop critical thinking when they are able to make predictions, build on previous knowledge, and see the connections between math concepts and the world around them.

Representation

Knowing that math is more than numbers on a page can help students construct meaning in mathematics. Students should be encouraged to represent a problem in a variety of ways. This might involve recognizing the same number whether it is written as a numeral, spoken as a word, or shown with objects. By providing a range of models to choose from, you will give your students the necessary tools to master all branches of mathematics.

Hands-On Math. If your students are having a hard time understanding a mathematical concept, why not give them a hand? A variety of manipulatives, such as base-ten blocks, linking cubes, or fraction stacks, can help students grasp the meaning of math concepts and offer a hands-on way to work with numbers. Some students need to experiment with objects in order to understand mathematical laws and properties.

Applying the process strands when teaching the basic skills for each area of mathematics will empower your students with critical-thinking skills, applicable to all areas of inquiry and exploration of the world around them.

Activity List

Activity 1–Shape Town

- **Standard:** Shapes
- **Goal:** Students will learn to recognize different shapes by using them to create something that will fit in with Shape Town.
- **Materials:** You will need construction paper, scissors, glue or paste, crayons, and assorted materials to decorate shapes.
- **Activity:** Give the students construction paper cutouts of different shapes. Each student will make something out of their shape to add to Shape Town, such as a house, tree, train, sun, etc. Then display them on a bulletin board.

Activity 2–Shape Museum

- **Standard:** Shapes
- **Goal:** Students will learn to recognize shapes by bringing in items from home that represent different shapes.
- **Materials:** None
- **Activity:** When learning about different shapes, have the kids bring in items from home that represent the different shapes. Display them on a table that allows the kids to touch and look at the different-shaped objects.

Activity 3–Magical Butterflies

- **Standard:** Symmetry
- **Goal:** Students will learn symmetry by creating a butterfly with the same design on each wing.
- **Materials:** You will need heavy paper, tempera paint, and scissors.
- **Activity:** Take a piece of heavy paper and fold it in half. Have the students quickly paint the paper on one side of the fold in different colors of tempera paint. Fold the paper again and rub on one side. Open the paper and let dry. When dry, fold the paper again and cut out a butterfly shape. When opened, it should be a magical butterfly with the same design on each side.

Activity 4–Silly Symmetry

- **Standard:** Symmetry
- **Goal:** Students will learn to make a symmetrical design out of their partner's original design.
- **Materials:** You will need pattern blocks.
- **Activity:** Have each student make a design using pattern blocks. Then pair up each student with a partner. Have them make a symmetrical design out their partner's original design.

Activity List

Activity 5–Race for Money

- **Standard:** Money
- **Goal:** Students will work together to combine coins to equal a predetermined value.
- **Materials:** You will need real coins, plastic coins, or large cutouts of coins.
- **Activity:** Place the students into two or more teams. Using real coins, plastic coins, or large cutouts of coins, give the students a money value and have each team work together to make a coin combination that equals that value. Then they must bring the coin combination to the teacher and the first team with a correct combination wins the round. Continue playing for desired number of rounds.

Activity 6–Beat the Calculator

- **Standard:** Addition/Subtraction
- **Goal:** Students will learn to solve addition and subtraction problems with a calculator and on their own.
- **Materials:** You will need addition and subtraction cards, a calculator, pencils, and paper.
- **Activity:** Divide the class into the "Calculator" team and the "Brain" team. Using addition or subtraction flash cards, the teacher will show one card at a time. The student who is up for that round on each team needs to solve the problem using a calculator for the "Calculator" team and their brain, pencil, and paper for the "Brain" team. The player who gets the answer first gains a point for their team. The first team to reach twenty points wins the game.

Activity 7–Roll 'Em

- **Standard:** Place value
- **Goal:** Students will learn place value by setting out base ten blocks to represent the numbers they rolled for tens and ones.
- **Materials:** You will need two number cubes (or die) and a set of base ten blocks for each set of partners of two in your class.
- **Activity:** Pair up students with a partner. Give each set of partners two number cubes (die) and a set of base ten blocks. Each player takes turns rolling one dice at a time. The first roll is for the tens and the second is for the ones. Have them set out the base ten blocks to represent the numbers rolled for tens and ones. The player with the higher or lower number, depending on if you are playing high or low, gets the point. The first player to get ten points wins the game.

Sample Test: Concepts

➡️ **Listen to your teacher read the problems below. Look at the pictures. Circle the correct answer for each problem.**

I. Which puppy is the second from the bone?

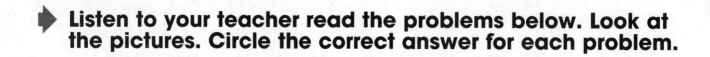

      a.   **b.**   **c.**   **d.**   **e.**

2. Look at the pattern. Which flower will come next?

  a.   **b.**   **c.**

3. Look at this number pattern. Which number goes in the blank?

    17, 18, 19, ____, 21, 22

a. 16

b. 20

c. 10

d. 23

4. Look at the number in the box. Which group of fish bowls is the same number?

7

STOP

0-7424-1941-X — *Using the Standards*

Sample Test: Addition and Subtraction

▶ **Solve each addition and subtraction problem. Circle "None of these" if the right answer is not given. Examples 1 and 2 are done for you.**

Examples

1. 7
    + 1

   a. 9
   (b.) 8
   c. 6
   d. None of these

2. 7
    − ☐
    1

   a. 7
   b. 9
   (c.) 6
   d. None of these

---

3. 6
    + 2

   a. 5
   b. 11
   c. 8
   d. None of these

6. 11
    − 9

   a. 2
   b. 19
   c. 20
   d. None of these

4. 5
    + 8

   a. 3
   b. 13
   c. 11
   d. None of these

7. 9
    − 4

   a. 4
   b. 13
   c. 5
   d. None of these

5. 4
    + 7

   a. 10
   b. 9
   c. 11
   d. None of these

8. 6
    − 1

   a. 4
   b. 7
   c. 3
   d. None of these

STOP

Sample Test: Geometry

➡ **Listen to your teacher read the problems. Look at the pictures. Circle the correct letter of the answer for each question. Example 1 is done for you.**

Example

1. Which one shows a triangle inside a square?

a.   (b.)   c.

2. How many sides does a rectangle have?
- **a.** 3
- **b.** 4
- **c.** 5
- **d.** 8

3. How many sides does a triangle have?
- **a.** 3
- **b.** 4
- **c.** 5
- **d.** 7

4. Look at the shape. How many sides are there?
- **a.** 5
- **b.** 8
- **c.** 7
- **d.** 4

5. Look at the shape. Look at the pictures. Which one is most like the shape?

a.

b.

c.

6. Look at the shapes in the box. How many circles do you count?

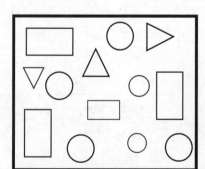

- **a.** 3
- **b.** 6
- **c.** 4
- **d.** 0

0-7424-1941-X — *Using the Standards*

Sample Test: Measurement

Listen to your teacher read the problems. Look at the pictures. Circle the correct answer for each question.

1. Look at the ruler. About how many inches is the pair of scissors?

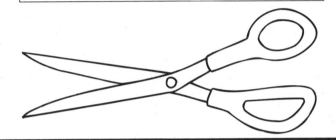

 a. 3

 b. 6

 c. 12

---

2. Gene wants to weigh himself. He would use a _____.

 a.   **b.**   **c.**

3. Josephine is making cookies. What will she use to measure flour?

 a.   **b.**    **c.**

4. Bonita can eat half a pizza. Which picture shows how much pizza she can eat?

 a.    **b.**    **c.**

STOP

0-7424-1941-X — *Using the Standards*

Small or Large?

➤ ◯ **Circle the smallest number in the shapes.**

▢ **Draw a square around the largest number.**

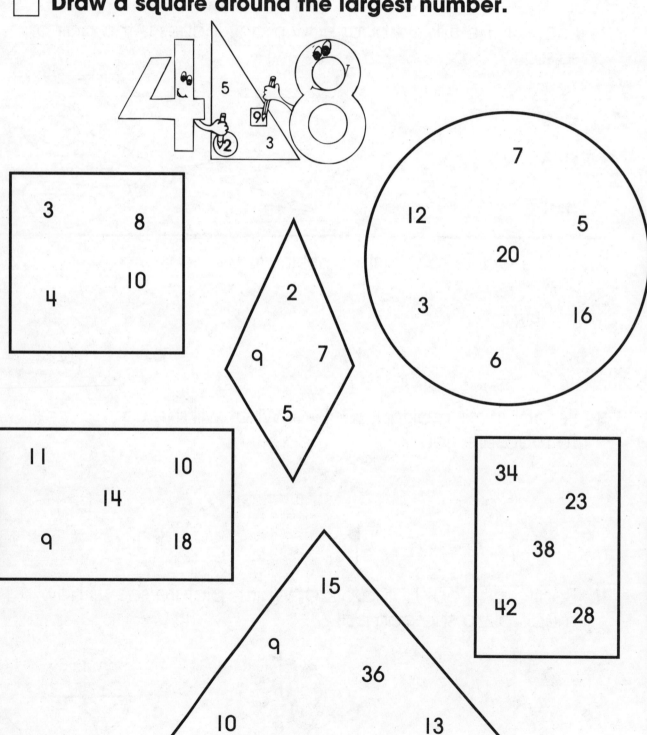

Square: 3, 8, 10, 4

Diamond: 2, 9, 7, 5

Circle: 7, 12, 5, 20, 3, 16, 6

Rectangle (left): 11, 10, 14, 9, 18

Rectangle (right): 34, 23, 38, 42, 28

Triangle: 15, 9, 36, 10, 13

0-7424-1941-X — Using the Standards

Name _____ Date _____

My Favorite Snacks

➤ **Add these numbers and write the answers on each snack.**

1.
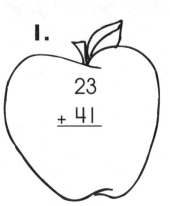
23
+ 41

2.
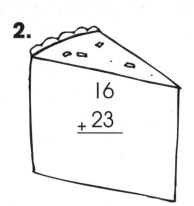
16
+ 23

3.
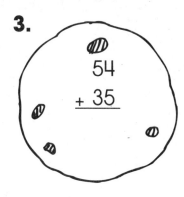
54
+ 35

4.
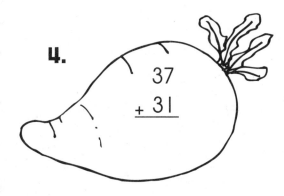
37
+ 31

5.
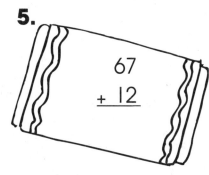
67
+ 12

6.
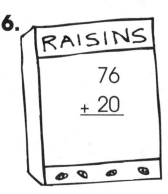
RAISINS
76
+ 20

7.
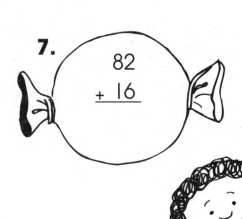
82
+ 16

8.

25
+ 53

9.
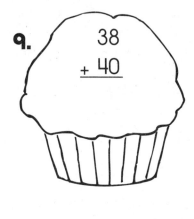
38
+ 40

Stepping Out

▶ **Look at the pictures of the caterpillars and spiders. Write the number of caterpillars for tens and the number of spiders for ones. Then, write the whole number on the line below.**

Key

= tens   = ones

1. _____
   tens   ones

   _____

2. _____
   tens   ones

   _____

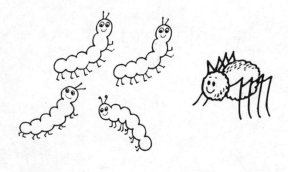

3. _____
   tens   ones

   _____

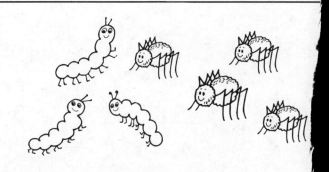

4. _____
   tens   ones

   _____

Yummy!

▶ **Match the treat before the ordinal numbers to the treats with numbers around the page. Use that number to find and circle the ordinal number for each treat. The first one is done for you.**

1.

2.

3.

4.

16.

a. third, sixteenth, (fifth)

b. fifteenth, fourth, first

5.

15.

c. twelfth, second, seventh

d. third, eleventh, fifteenth

6.

14.

e. eighth, first, tenth

f. sixteenth, thirteenth, third

7.

13.

g. ninth, second, thirteenth

h. sixth, seventh, ninth

8.

12.

11.

10.

9.

Name _____ Date _____

Picture Fractions

$\frac{1}{2}$ = 1 out of 2 equal groups

▶ **Draw a star next to the sets that show $\frac{1}{2}$.**

1.

2.

3.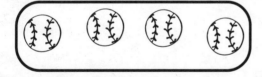

4.

5.

6.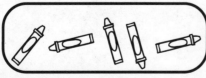

0-7424-1941-X — Using the Standard

How Many Toys?

Read the story problems. Write the answers on the lines.

1. Pete has 3 trucks, 2 balls, and 1 bear to trade. How many toys does Pete have in all to trade?

 _____

2. Colin has 1 bear, 7 balls, and 2 cars. Colin traded Pete 2 cars for his truck. How many toys does Colin have now?

 _____

3. Melissa has 6 dolls. She also brought 5 bears. How many toys did she bring in all?

 _____

4. Melissa gave Kitty 2 of her 6 dolls. Kitty gave Melissa 1 ball. How many dolls does Melissa have left?

 _____

5. Trin has 4 bears. She has 1 baseball and 1 jump rope. How many toys does Trin want to trade in all?

 _____

Farm Life

➤ Add the numbers. Write your answers.

1. 25
    + 32

2. 15
    + 11

3. 81
    + 10

4. 72
    + 17

5. 10
    + 60

6. 28
    + 61

7. 61
    + 26

8. 62
    + 36

9. 33
    + 42

10. 14
     + 54

11. 14
     + 41

12. 35
     + 43

13. 12
     + 21

14. 25
     + 32

15. 37
     + 22

16. 45
     + 14

17. 19
     + 20

0-7424-1941-X — *Using the Standard*

Name _____ Date _____

Springtime

Subtract the numbers. Write your answers.

1.   64
      − 40

2.   87
      − 12

3.   81
      − 21

4.   48
      − 27

5.   70
      − 20

6.   66
      − 33

7.   28
      − 15

8.   98
      − 54

9.   86
      − 82

10.   74
       − 52

11.   78
       − 62

12.   35
       − 25

13.   94
       − 43

14.   49
       − 20

15.   59
       − 16

16.   45
       + 14

17.   88
       − 10

Prediction and Probability Beads

➡ **Color the square beads one color and the round beads another color. Then answer the questions below.**

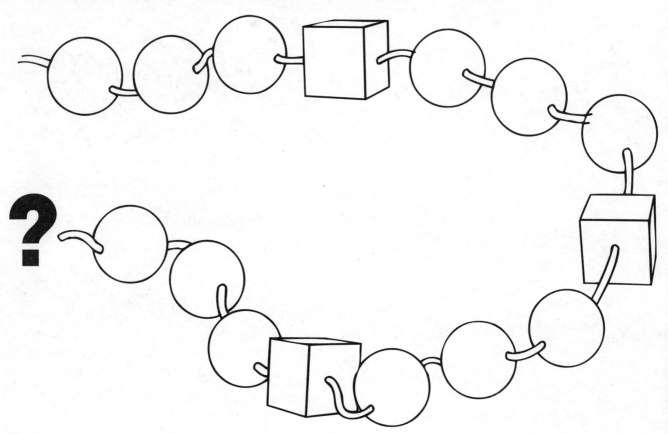

1. Look for the question mark (?) above. Which bead do you think should be in this spot? _____

Why? _____

_____

2. If the beads were mixed together in a bag and you reached in and pulled one out, which shape bead do you think it would be? _____

Why? _____

_____

Finding Patterns

Look at each pattern. Find the missing picture on the right. Draw a line to connect them. Not all the pictures will be used.

1.

2.

3.

4.

5.

6.

A Summer Picnic

➤ **Use math to be sure that you have enough food and a place to sit for 12 people at the picnic. Draw pictures to show your answers.**

1. There are 8 hot dogs in a package. Grandpa wants there to be enough hot dogs so everyone can have 2.

How many packages does he need to bring? _____

2. Aunt Lottie is baking cookies for the picnic. Her recipe for a batch of cookies makes 24 cookies. She wants everyone to be able to have 3 cookies.

If she bakes 1 batch of cookies, will she have enough?

_____

3. Our neighbor is going to bring blankets to spread on the ground for everyone to sit on while they eat. She thinks 4 people will fit on each blanket.

How many blankets does she need to bring? _____

4. My friend's mom is going to bring fruit for everyone. She plans to bring bananas and peaches. She decided to bring the same number of each kind of fruit. She would like to have 1 piece of fruit for each person, plus 4 extra pieces in case someone is really hungry.

How many bananas and peaches should my friend's mom bring? _____

0-7424-1941-X — *Using the Standar*

Bouncing Balls

Study the drawings below. They represent equations. Using pictures to show a multiplication problem helps you to solve it.

This drawing shows 3 x 5 = 15

This drawing shows 5 x 3 = 15

Draw a picture for each problem using circles. Write the answer for each problem in the box.

I. 4 x 3 = ☐

2. 6 x 4 = ☐

3. 5 x 4 = ☐

4. 5 x 6 = ☐

5. 3 x 4 = ☐

6. 3 x 7 = ☐

Green Jelly Beans

➤ **Use green, yellow, and red crayons or pencils to color the jelly beans. Then answer the questions below.**

1. What color do you have the most of? _____

least of? _____

2. If you reached into the jar and took a handful of jelly beans, what color would most of them be? _____

Why? _____

A Bear in the Woods

Use the graph to answer the questions.

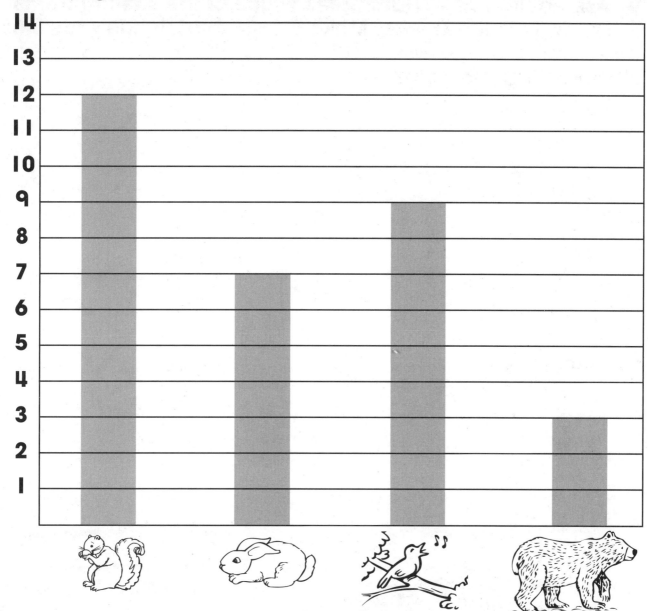

1. Are there more squirrels or birds? _____

2. Are there more rabbits or bears? _____

3. Are there more birds or rabbits? _____

4. Are there more rabbits or squirrels? _____

Special Treats

▶ **Ask each of your classmates which of the special treats below is their favorite. Make a tally mark in the drawings to record everyone's favorite. What did you discover from collecting this data?**

0-7424-1941-X — *Using the Standar*

Special Treats (cont.)

▶ **Mark your tally marks for each treat from page 86 in this pictograph. What was the treat that had the most tally marks? What had the fewest?**

Ship Shapes

▶ **Color the picture. . .**   **Match. . .**

△ green

□ red

○ yellow

□ orange

〰 blue

circle   **1.** △

square   **2.** □

triangle   **3.** ○

rectangle   **4.** □

The Shape of Things

Color the shapes in each row that are the same size and shape. Write **T** for triangle, **R** for rectangle, and **S** for square on the lines. The first row is done for you.

T _____   R _____   T _____   T _____

1. _____   _____   _____   _____

2. _____   _____   _____

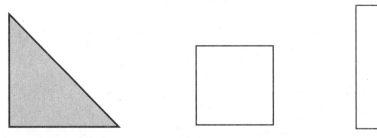

3. _____   _____   _____   _____

Square Roses

Pick a color and color one triangle. Color all the other triangles that are the same size with the same color.

Pick a different color. Color another set of triangles that are the same size.

Repeat with a different color for each different size of triangles.

Name _____   Date _____

Calculating Caterpillars

➤ **How long is each caterpillar? Count the sections. Write your answer on the line. Use the chart to find what color to color each caterpillar.**

Length	Color
1–2	green
3–4	yellow
5–6	orange
7–8	red

1.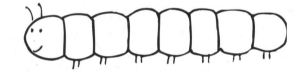

_____

_____

2.

_____

_____

3.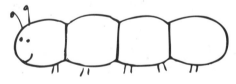

_____

_____

4.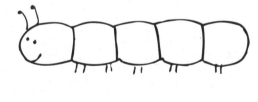

_____

_____

5.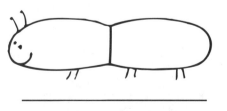

_____

_____

6.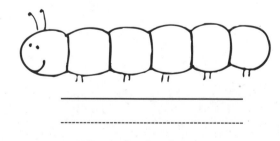

_____

_____

Helping Out

➤ **Hildy's Youth Club poured glasses of water at their town's annual River Run race. Use the drawings to help you answer the questions. Choose one of the three choices below each question.**

I cup   2 cups   2 pints
                I pint   I quart

1. Hildy's club poured 40 cups of water. They gave away 36 cups. How much was left?

    I cup   I pint   I quart

2. In 30 minutes, the kids in the club gave away 2 quarts of water. How many cups did they give away?

    2 cups   4 cups   8 cups

3. One runner drank I cup during the race. He drank 3 more cups after the race. How much did he drink in all?

    I pint   4 pints   I quart

4. Terry spilled 8 cups of water during the race. How much did he spill?

    4 pints   4 quarts   I quart

0-7424-1941-X — Using the Standard

It's Time for Vacation!

➡️ **Read and solve the story problems. Use the calendars for help.**

June

S	M	T	W	Th	F	Sa
					1	2
3	4	5	6	7	8	9
10	11	12	13	14	15	16
17	18	19	20	21	22	23
24	25	26	27	28	29	30

July

S	M	T	W	Th	F	Sa
1	2	3	4	5	6	7
8	9	10	11	12	13	14
15	16	17	18	19	20	21
22	23	24	25	26	27	28
29	30	31				

1. Yasir went to camp for 2 weeks. How many days was he gone?

_____

2. Seth missed 61 days of school when his family moved to this country. About how many months did he miss?

_____

3. Ricardo's tennis camp met from June 1 to July 31? How many months was Ricardo at camp?

_____

4. During vacation, Carter read for 72 hours. If he had read all that time at once, how many days would he have read?

_____

5. Elenora went on vacation for 2 weeks in July and 2 weeks in December. How many months in all did Elenora vacation?

_____

6. Ajay and Reva waited at the airport for 15 minutes. What part of an hour did they wait?

_____

0-7424-1941-X — *Using the Standards*

Space Travel

▶ **Use an inch ruler to measure how far each rocket will fly to reach the target planet. Write the measurement on the line.**

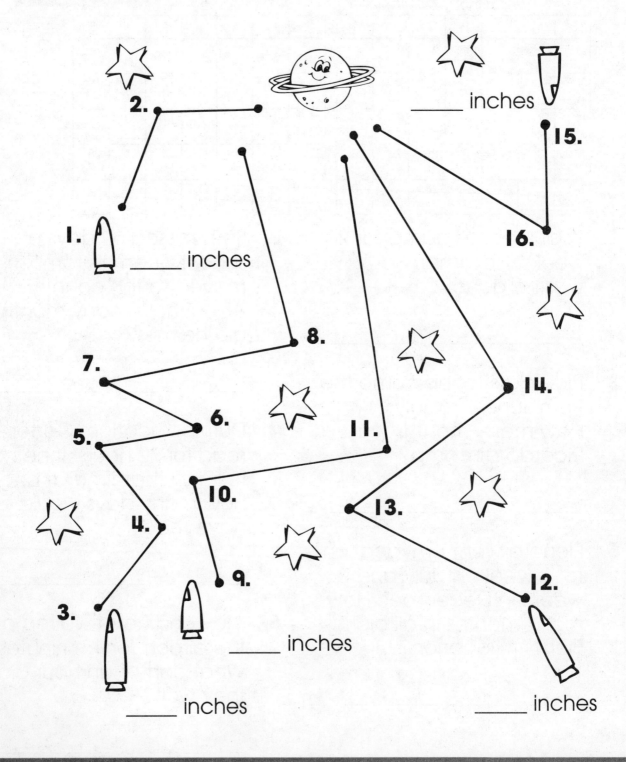

_____ inches

_____ inches

_____ inches

_____ inches

_____ inches

Weather Watch

> **Look at the temperature in each thermometer.**
> **Write the temperature and hot, cold, or mild**
> **on the lines to tell what kind of day it is.**

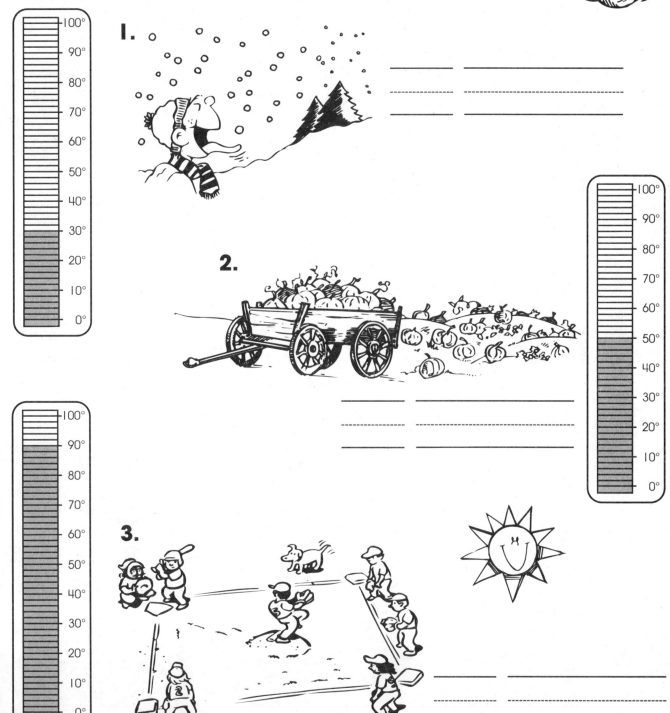

1.

_____ _____

------------- ------------------------

_____ _____

2.

_____ _____

------------- ------------------------

_____ _____

3.

_____ _____

------------- ------------------------

_____ _____

Time to Go!

▶ **Kerry has a busy day. Look at her schedule. Look at the six clocks. Write the correct time on the first line under the clock. Then write the activity on the second line.**

10:30 A.M.	shop
11:00 A.M.	soccer
1:00 P.M.	read
3:30 P.M.	party
5:00 P.M.	dinner
8:00 P.M.	bath

1. _____

   _____

2. _____

   _____

3. _____

   _____

4. _____

   _____

5. _____

   _____

6. _____

   _____

0-7424-1941-X — *Using the Standar*

Counting Coins

Count the money. Write the amount on the line.

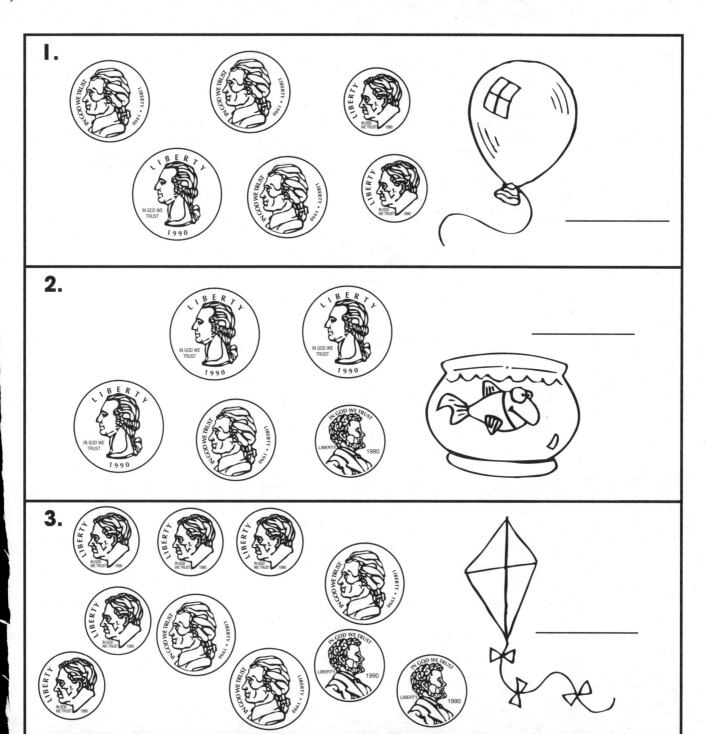

1. _____

2. _____

3. _____

Arctic Animals

▶ **Make a graph of the arctic animals. Color one space for each animal.**

➡ **Use the graph you made of the arctic animals on page 98 to answer these questions.**

1. How many are there? _____

2. How many are there? _____

3. How many are there? _____

4. How many are there? _____

5. Which animal appeared the most in the picture according to your graph? Circle its picture.

6. Which animal appeared the fewest times in the picture according to your graph? Circle its picture.

7. How many more are there than ?

8. How many fewer are there than ?

Standards in Science

Science means exploration, whether it involves classroom experiments or field trips. A standards-based science curriculum recognizes that a vital part of science education is active exploration and discovery. The National Science Teachers Association (**www.nsta.org**) has developed a series of resources called *Pathways to the Science Standards* to guide student learning in science. NSTA divides science knowledge into the following areas:

- Science as Inquiry
- Physical Science
- Life Science
- Earth and Space Science
- Science and Technology
- Science in Personal and Social Perspectives
- History and Nature of Science

At all levels of inquiry, students should work through the scientific process. Identify the hypothesis or concept to be tested; perform an experiment; collect data; interpret the results; summarize the findings.

Space for Science. With a limited amount of resources available, how can you create the best possible science environment for your students? A sturdy plastic science cart can be a wonderful addition to your classroom. Fill the cart with tools for scientific inquiry—clipboards with paper for recording observations, thermometers, scales, microscope, containers, string, rulers, calculators, and nature samples. After presenting a question to your class, allow them to select their own materials to test the hypothesis. This encourages active learning and saves space too!

An increased understanding of science as a process of exploration will lead students naturally to cross-curricular endeavors. Science is linked to math in recording and reporting data; to language arts in communicating the findings; to social studies in understanding the ways scientific discoveries change life for people and cultures.

Activity 1–Animal Guessing Game

- **Standard:** Understanding animal attributes
- **Goal:** Students will learn to identify animals by guessing clues of their attributes.
- **Materials:** You will need pictures of animals and tape.
- **Activity:** Tape a picture of an animal to each student's back. The students will walk around the classroom asking their classmates yes or no questions about their animal. When the students correctly guess their animal, they move the animal to their front. Continue playing until all students figure out their animals.

Activity 2–Name That Animal

- **Standard:** Understanding animal attributes
- **Goal:** Students will learn to identify animals by listing clues of their attributes and guessing the animals of their classmates.
- **Materials:** You will need large construction paper and something for the students to draw with, such as crayons or markers.
- **Activity:** Students will pick an animal and list clues on a large piece of construction paper that would help their classmates guess their animal. They should include characteristics and specific descriptions of their animal on the front of the paper. On the back, they should draw a picture of their animal. Either as a whole group or with students walking around the room, have the students guess their classmates' animals.

Activity 3–Plants At Work

- **Standard:** Understanding plant attributes
- **Goal:** Students will learn what each part of a plant is and what its purpose is to help the plant survive.
- **Materials:** You will need paper and pencils.
- **Activity:** Discuss with the students what each part of a plant does to help the plant survive. Brainstorm as a class examples of jobs in the community that perform similar functions (example—a leaf makes food, so it could be the plant's restaurant). Have the students make diagrams of a plant with the community jobs included.

Activity 4–Tasty "Tree"ts

- **Standard:** Understanding plant attributes
- **Goal:** Students will learn what each part of a plant is and what its purpose is to help the plant survive.
- **Materials:** You will need edible parts of plants, such as fruits, leafy vegetables, beans, celery, etc.
- **Activity:** Supply different edible parts of plants, such as fruits, leafy vegetables, beans, celery, etc. Hold up each food item and have the students decide which part of the plant it is and its purpose for the plant.

Sample Test: Science

➡️ **Listen to your teacher read the story and the questions. Listen to each answer choice. Circle the letter of the best answer for the question. Example I is done for you.**

Example

Pollution Control

We need our earth. When air, water, or land is dirty, it is called polluted. Smoke gets in the air. Trash pollutes the land. Chemicals get in the water. We must work to keep the earth clean.

I. How can we care for the earth?

   a. Keep it clean.

   b. Put smoke in the air.

   c. Throw trash out the window.

The Splendor of Fall

Fall is the season after summer. The days are shorter and it is dark longer.

It can be cool in the fall. Some leaves change color and fall to the ground. Some plants stop growing. Other plants die. Fruit and vegetables get ripe and people pick them.

Animals change too. Some find safe places to sleep all winter. Other animals change color. Some go to warmer places until spring comes back.

2. When does fall come?
   a. after summer
   b. after winter
   c. before spring

3. What happens to some leaves?
   a. They grow bigger.
   b. They change color.
   c. Some become flowers.

4. Why do people pick fruit in the fall?
   a. It is ripe.
   b. It is rotten.
   c. The fruit is sour.

5. Why do some animals go to a warmer place?
   a. to sleep
   b. to hide from dogs
   c. to stay warm

Sample Test: Science

▶ **Listen to your teacher read the story and the questions. Listen to each answer choice. Circle the letter of the best answer for the question. Example I is done for you.**

Example

Mammals

Mammals are a group of animals. Most mammals have hair or fur. They move by walking, running, swimming, or flying. Mother mammals feed their babies milk. One mammal is a dog. Another is a whale. Humans are mammals, too!

I. What do mother mammals feed their babies?

   a. carrots

   b. milk

   c. hot dogs

Liquid Matter

All things are made of matter. Liquid is a kind of matter.

Liquid has mass. That means it takes up space. Liquid can take many shapes like a puddle of water and a cup of water. Both are liquid, but they look different!

Some liquid is thick, like maple syrup. Some liquid is thin and runny, like milk and water. Liquid can be hot, like coffee, or cold, like milk. You can see, touch, and even taste some liquids.

2. What are all things made of?
   a. some kind of matter
   b. wind
   c. ice

3. What does mass mean?
   a. It is cool.
   b. It takes up space.
   c. It can freeze.

4. Name a thin and runny liquid.
   a. syrup
   b. ice
   c. milk

5. What is a liquid you can taste?
   a. bark
   b. air
   c. orange juice

Animal Attributes

▶ **Circle the correct name for each animal.**

1.

turtle

tadpole

2.

goose

chicken

3.

beaver

raccoon

4.

bird

bat

5.

eel

snake

▶ **Which of the animals above hatch from eggs? Write them on the lines.**

_____

_____

_____

_____

_____

_____

_____

 0-7424-1941-X — *Using the Standard*

Will It Float?

➡ **Cut out the pictures and paste each one in the correct place.**

Things That Will Float

Things That Will Sink

rock

feather

stick

nail

spoon

leaf

egg

paper

What Are Clouds?

➡ **Cut out the pictures. Paste them in the correct order to show the cycle of how clouds are made.**

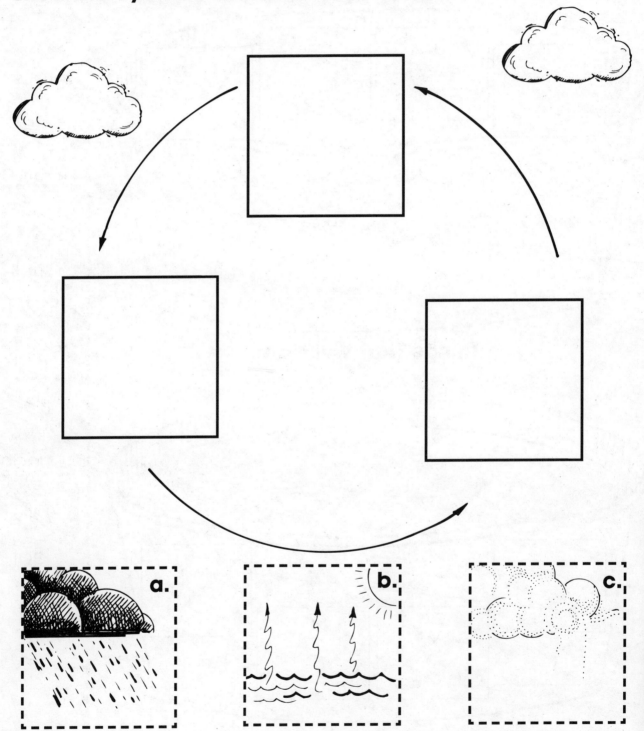

All Types of Matter

➡️ **Put an X on the thing that does not belong in each set. Write solids, liquids, or gases to tell how the others in the set are alike.**

1. _____
   _____

2. _____

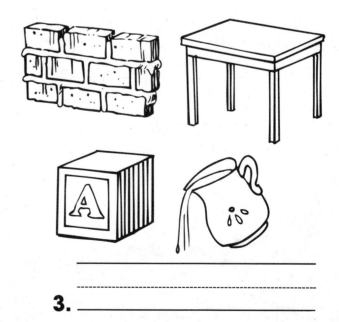

3. _____

Animal Kingdom

➡ **Use the Word Box to write the name of each animal. Write the code number in the circle to tell where each animal lives.**

Word Box

bee	bird	pig
cow	fish	penguin

Code
1—land
2—sea
3—air

1. _____
_____
_____

2. _____
_____
_____

3. _____
_____
_____

4. _____
_____
_____

5. _____
_____
_____

6. _____
_____
_____

Animal Babies

➤ **Draw a line to match each animal parent with its baby. Use the Word Box to write each baby's name**

Word Box: kitten   lamb   piglet   duckling

1.

a. _____

2.

b. _____

3.

c. _____

4.

d. _____

Standards in Social Studies

Social studies encourages students to be full and active participants in the world around them through an ever-increasing understanding of their community, state, country, and world. The National Council for the Social Studies (NCSS) standards can be found at: **www.socialstudies.org/standards**. The NCSS lists ten thematic strands:

- Culture
- Time, Continuity, and Change
- People, Places, and Environment
- Individual Development and Identity
- Individuals, Groups, and Institutions
- Power, Authority, and Governance
- Production, Distribution, and Consumption
- Science, Technology, and Society
- Global Connections
- Civic Ideals and Practices

Use the broad spectrum of knowledge covered by social studies to develop your own thematic cross-curricular units. Social studies exploration naturally lends itself to other subjects: reading more about a people or place, using math to interpret data, drawing on scientific principles to understand climate and environment, and tapping into language arts skills to report what has been discovered.

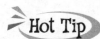

Theme-Based Learning in Social Studies. Take full advantage of the cross-curricular possibilities of social studies by creating richly textured theme-based units for your students. Students working through a unit on the Amazon might do all of the following in different subject areas:

- read books and stories about the rainforest;
- learn new vocabulary as they study the layers of the rainforest;
- interpret data about animals or people by reading graphs and charts;
- discover the location of the Amazon by looking at maps;
- examine the main exports and make a graph to communicate this data;
- use scientific evidence to understand the climate of the region;
- become involved citizens as they learn about conservation efforts.

Thematic units provide a dynamic way to connect learning across the curriculum areas and to deepen student connections to the world around them.

Activity List

 Activity 1–Wants and Needs
- **Standard:** Identifying the basic vocabulary of economics
- **Goal:** Students will learn to identify things that people need, as opposed to want, in today's world.
- **Materials:** You will need magazines, scissors, glue or paste, and poster board.
- **Activity:** Have students look through magazines and find things that are wants (toys, vacations, etc.) and needs (food, shelter, etc.). Make class posters using the things the students identified as wants and needs.

 Activity 2–Super Shoppers
- **Standard:** Identifying the basic vocabulary of economics
- **Goal:** Students will learn that different people have different economic wants, which is why there are so many products available.
- **Materials:** You will need magazines, scissors, glue or paste, paper, and something for the students to draw with, such as crayons or markers, and large construction paper.
- **Activity:** Students will cut pictures out of magazines or draw pictures of things they want (their economic wants). Each student will arrange and glue their pictures onto a large piece of construction paper. When students are finished, have them compare and contrast what they each have on their posters. Discuss how different people have different economic wants, which is why there are so many products available today.

 Activity 3–Trading Day
- **Standard:** Identifying the basic vocabulary of economics
- **Goal:** Students will learn how people used to trade for goods and services instead of using money to purchase them.
- **Materials:** No school supplies needed
- **Activity:** Have students bring in one or two toys from home that they no longer want (and have permission from a parent to trade). Discuss with the students how people in the past would trade goods and services. Have the students participate in trading their toys, pointing out that each of them could end up with something they really want that the original owner did not want anymore.

 Activity 4–Treasure Hunt
- **Standard:** Working with maps
- **Goal:** Students will learn to use a map to get to a certain location.
- **Materials:** You will need paper and pen to draw maps, write directions, and buy "treasures."
- **Activity:** Make a map of the school or playground and make copies for the class. Put the students into groups. Give each group a map with directions from the classroom to another location on the map. When the group gets to the location on the map, there should be another map waiting there for them. They will need to follow that map to another location. After a couple of locations, have a treasure waiting for the students.

Sample Test: Social Studies

➡️ **Listen to your teacher read the story and the question. Listen to each answer choice. Circle the letter of the best answer for the question. Example I is done for you.**

Example

Food Facts

Food is important. It helps keep us alive. People eat many different things. Some like meat. They might eat beef, chicken, or pork. Some people eat only vegetables. They are called vegetarians.

They like carrots, potatoes, and broccoli. Many people eat grains and fruits.

1. What might a vegetarian eat?
   a. chicken
   b. beef
   c. carrots

Three Friends

My name is Evan. I live in a yellow house. I have two brothers. My mom stays at home with us. Dad is a truck driver. I have a dog.

My name is Sergio. I was born in Mexico. I live with my grandparents. We have three cats. I love school. Science is my best subject.

I am Nicole. I live with my mother. We have a nice apartment. She makes pretty cakes at the bakery. Sometimes we go to see movies together. I have fun visiting my dad on weekends.

2. How many brothers does Evan have?
   a. three
   b. none
   c. two

3. Who was born in Mexico?
   a. Nicole
   b. Sergio
   c. Evan

4. Why might Nicole visit her dad on weekends?
   a. He does not live with her.
   b. She goes to the movies.
   c. She lives with her grandparents.

Sample Test: Social Studies

▶ **Listen to your teacher read the story and the questions. Listen to all of the answer choices. Circle the letter of the best answer for the question. Example 1 is done for you.**

Example

Changing Times

We went to visit my grandmother. Dad said it looks very different around his old home. One thing that is different is the neighborhood. There used to be woods around the houses. He would play in them. Now there are more people and new houses. There is even a new park!

1. What is one change in the neighborhood?
   a. a new park
   (b.) more woods
   c. stormy weather

How to Get There

A map is a picture of a place. It can be of the whole world. It can show a city or even your school. The very first maps were made from dirt, sand, or clay. Now maps are on paper, computer and TV screens, and globes.

People make maps to help them remember where things are. Long ago, people made maps to help them remember where there was water or food. Now maps are made to show the way to a place. Some maps show where there are rivers, lakes, and mountains.

2. What is a map?
   a. a picture of a place
   b. a car
   c. a way to find phone numbers

3. What were the first maps made of?
   a. computers
   b. dirt, clay, and sand
   c. water

4. Why would you need a map?
   a. to find the way to a place
   b. to catch a bug
   c. for playing cards

In America, We Are Free To...

▶ **Cut out the boxes below and paste them where "what we are free to do" matches the picture.**

---

a. say what we feel

b. worship any way we wish

c. pick the work we want to do

d. write what we think

0-7424-1941-X — *Using the Standa*

Our Constitution

The United States has a set of **laws**. It is called the **Constitution**. It lists our **rights** and **freedoms**. The Constitution was written over **200 years** ago. You can see the Constitution in **Washington, D.C.**

► **Color the scrolls with words from above that tell about our Constitution.**

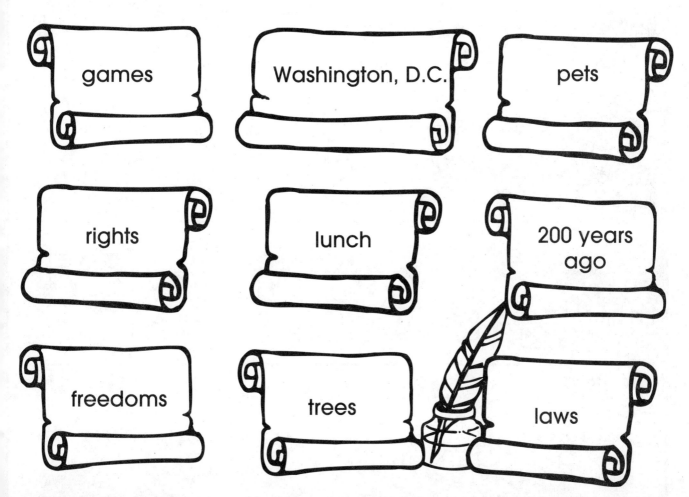

games

Washington, D.C.

pets

rights

lunch

200 years ago

freedoms

trees

laws

Money Earned

▶ **Phoebe earned some money by helping out a neighbor. Count her money. Circle the most expensive item Phoebe can buy at each store with the money she has.**

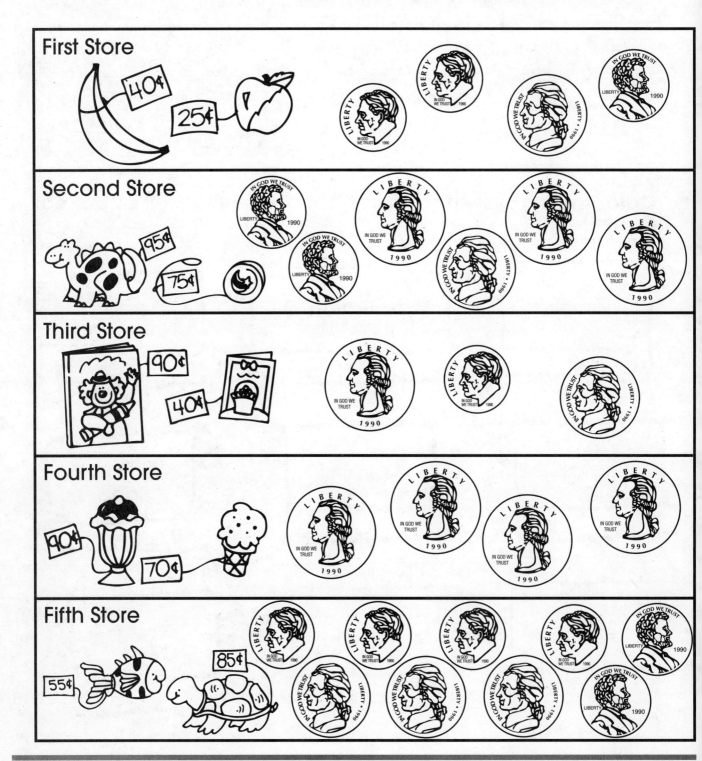

First Store — banana 40¢, apple 25¢

Second Store — dinosaur 95¢, yo-yo 75¢

Third Store — clown book 90¢, picture 40¢

Fourth Store — sundae 90¢, ice cream cone 70¢

Fifth Store — fish 55¢, turtle 85¢

0-7424-1941-X — *Using the Standards*

What Is a Globe?

A **globe** is a map of the earth. It is shaped like a ball. So is the earth. A globe shows where all the lands and oceans are. It shows where the North Pole and the South Pole are. The North Pole is near the top of the globe. The South Pole is near the bottom.

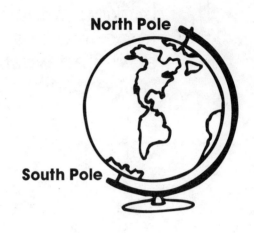

North Pole

South Pole

➡ **Fill in the ◯ to answer yes or no.**

		Yes	No
1.	A globe is a map of the stars.	◯	◯
2.	A globe is a map of the earth.	◯	◯
3.	The North Pole is near the top of the globe.	◯	◯
4.	The South Pole is near the top of the globe.	◯	◯
5.	A globe shows only oceans.	◯	◯
6.	A globe is shaped like a ball.	◯	◯
7.	A globe shows oceans and land.	◯	◯
8.	The Earth is shaped like a box.	◯	◯

Name _____   Date _____

Asking Directions

Looking at the directions on a map can tell you which way to go. The four main directions on a map are **north**, **south**, **east**, and **west**. On most maps, north is at the top; south is at the bottom; east is to the right; and west is to the left.

North

West   East

South

▶ Write on the lines what you think the correct direction is.

1. The [tree house] is _____ _____ of the [girl on swing] .

2. The [person tumbling] is _____ _____ of the [tree house] .

3. The [trees] are _____ _____ of the [person tumbling] .

4. The [girl on swing] is _____ _____ of the [trees] .

Thomas Edison

• • • • • • • • • • • • ▶ Thomas Edison was an inventor. He made new things. He also made other people's inventions better. His ideas changed the way people lived.

▶ **Draw a line from the picture of an invention that changed the way people lived to the picture showing how it is or was used.**

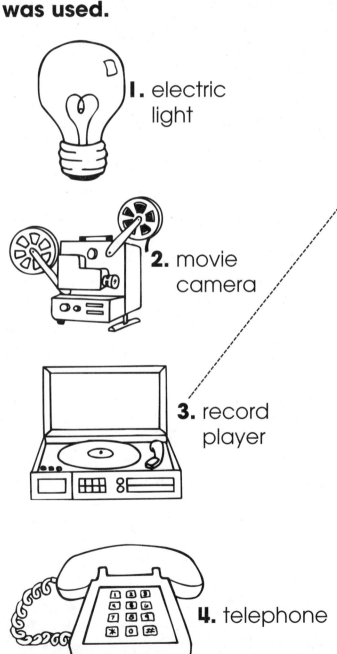

1. electric light

2. movie camera

3. record player

4. telephone

a.

b.

c.

d.

0-7424-1941-X — *Using the Standards*

Where Do You Live?

▶ **Look at the different kinds of neighborhoods. Cut out the different kinds of houses where people live at the bottom of the page and paste them next to the right neighborhoods.**

			1.
			2.
			3.
			4.

 a.
 b.
 c.
 d.

0-7424-1941-X — *Using the Standards*

Name _____ Date _____

Finding Friends on the Map

⮞ **When friends or relatives move to a different part of the country, you can find their city, state, or both on a map.**

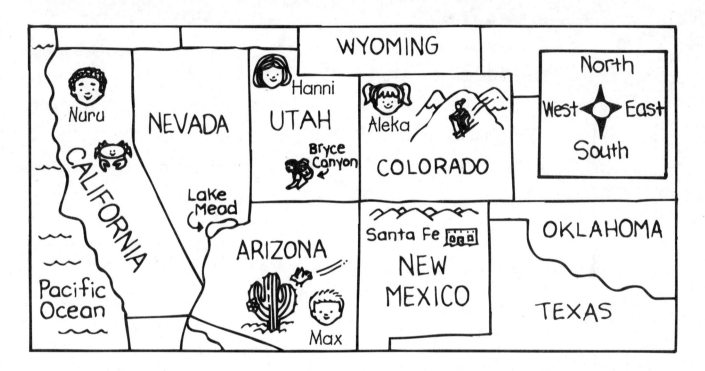

1. Color the state **west** of Nevada blue.

2. Color the state **south** of Utah red.

3. Color the state **north** of New Mexico green.

4. Color the state **east** of Nevada purple.

5. Color the other states yellow.

Finding Friends on the Map (cont.)

➡ **Four children wrote stories about their friends. Read the stories. Look for clues. Use the map on page 121. Then answer the questions below.**

Aleka's Friend

6. One hot day, my friend walked to the beach. He waded into the water. Then he yelled, "Ouch!" A little crab pinched his big toe.

What is the setting?

a. _____

Who is Aleka's friend?

b. _____

Max's Friend

7. My friend put on hiking boots and filled a water bottle. She and her mom hiked into Bryce Canyon to see the pretty rocks.

What is the setting?

a. _____

Who is Max's friend?

b. _____

Nuru's Friend

8. My friend has a special animal home in his backyard. It is a huge cactus. It has big arms. Lots of birds make nests in holes in the arms. My friend likes to watch the birds.

What is the setting?

a. _____

Who is Nuru's friend?

b. _____

Hanni's Friend

9. My friend's birthday was fun. She learned to snowboard. Her family drove to the mountains. It was cold. There was a lot of snow. She learned to slide down the hills.

What is the setting?

a. _____

Who is Hanni's friend?

b. _____

Reading

**Sample Test:
  Word Analysis................17**
3. d   **4.** b   **5.** b   **6.** c

Sample Test: Vocabulary.....18
3. c   **4.** a   **5.** b   **6.** a
7. c   **8.** b   **9.** a   **10.** c

**Sample Test:
  Comprehension................19**
2. c   **3.** a   **4.** a   **5.** b

**Sample Test:
  Comprehension................20**
1. b   **2.** a   **3.** c   **4.** b

Name That Picture 21
1. s   **2.** c   **3.** s
4. b   **5.** p   **6.** b
7. g   **8.** l   **9.** c
10. d   **11.** g   **12.** d
13. z   **14.** s   **15.** g

Snack Pack 22
1. g   **2.** t
3. r   **4.** k   **5.** x
6. p   **7.** t   **8.** t
9. t   **10.** g   **11.** d
12. k   **13.** n   **14.** x

Which Whale? 23
1. Where
2. Which
3. whale
4. When
5. wheel

Let It Snow 24
1. friend
2. cream
3. treat
4. grow
pl—plant, plug
fl—flag, flake

What to Do at the Zoo?........25
snake—bake, wake
bear—care, wear
kangaroo—too, you
seal—feel, meal

Compound Kittens 26
compound words—blueberry,
fireplace, barnyard, goldfish,
cowboy, without, popcorn,
grandmother
not compound words (X)—my
room, with you

We're Happy! 27
he is—he's
it is—it's
she is—she's
they are—they're
you are—you're

Chirp, Chirp.........................28
1. bang
2. chirp
3. gulp
4. crash
5. boom
6. pop

My Backyard 29
1. sun
2. kite
3. ball
4. dog
5. cat

Circus Fun...........................30
Synonyms (colored yellow)

laughed, giggled
watched, stared
pretty, beautiful
always, forever

Not Synonyms (colored red)
above, below
clapped, watched

Growing Up 31
1. big
2. hot
3. new
4. up
5. play

A Day at the Park.................32
1. picture on the left
2. picture on the right
3. picture on the right
4. picture on the left
5. picture on the left

Owls Hoot 33
Nouns—rabbits, children, dog,
sun, lunch, bedroom
Verbs—play, barks, sleep, hop,
shines, eat

How Are You?......................34
1. is
2. am
3. is
4. are
5. am
6. are

Tyrone Turtle 35

The Big Top 36
1. A big flag is on the circus tent.
2. The little boy has two balloons.
3. The circus clown is wearing funny shoes.
4. The elephant likes to eat peanuts.
5. The woman is holding cotton candy.

Sky Blue 37
Answers will vary.

The Lion and the Mouse .. 38–39
1. animals
2. make-believe
3. mouse
4. lion
5. He was not hungry.
6. She said she would help him.
Lion—big, roars, big paws
Mouse—small, squeaks, sharp teeth

Soft Woolly Lamb 40
1. white, fluffy
2. Two, noisy
3. old, torn
4. sweet, crisp
5. bright, warm
6. six, round

Uh-Oh! 41
1. d
2. b
3. a
4. c

Camping Trip 42
Sentences will vary.

Doghouse Duties 43
A. 1. Ralph's
2. doghouse
3. needs
4. painting.

B. 1. I
2. have
3. red
4. paint.

C. 1. Here
2. are
3. two
4. brushes.

D. 1. Ralph
2. is
3. very
4. happy.

What Do You Think? 44
1. a　　2. b

How Are You Feeling? 45
1. Lian
2. Carina
3. Bridget
4. Dermot
5. Johann
6. Carina
7. Bridget
8. Lian

You Can Make a Difference 46–47
1. It makes air unsafe to breathe.
2. Smoke causes air pollution. Cars cause air pollution.
3. People can plant more trees. People can find a safer way to burn fuel. People can drive their cars less.
4. To convince people that they can make a difference in fighting air pollution.

Important Lessons 48
1. Mr. Tortoise caught up and won the race.
2. When the bird started to sing she dropped the cheese. The fox got the cheese.

True Stories? 49
1. forest
2. outer space
Real stories could take place in both of the settings.

Language Arts

Sample Test: Mechanics 53
3. b
4. b
5. c
6. a

Sample Test: Usage 54
3. b
4. a
5. c
6. c
7. c
8. b

Sample Test: Sentences 55
3. b
4. a
5. c
6. c
7. c
8. a

Sample Test: Paragraphs 56
2. a
3. b
4. b
5. b

I'm Having Fun! 57
1. I have a new bike. It is blue.
2. We are selling fruit. We have a fruit stand.
3. I have a new dog. I got him at the Pet Shop.
4. I love my doll. Her name is Marcie.

Where's My Cave? 58
1. period
2. question mark
3. period
4. question mark
5. period
6. period

Summer Vacation 59
1. How was your vacation?
2. Where did you go?
3. Did you ride in a train or a car?
4. How long was your trip?
5. Did you take pictures?

By the Sea 60
1. ate
2. two
3. road
4. I
5. see

Fish Swim 61
1. The stars shine.
2. An airplane flies.
3. The top spins.
4. The baby smiled.
5. A duck quacks.

Making Sense 62
1. My mom likes her job.
2. Two sheep ran down the hill.
3. Our school had a bake sale.
4. Toshi bought some candy.
5. My class went to the Art Museum.
Other endings for sentences will vary.

Honey Bee 63
1. kros—cross
2. graid—grade
3. graz—grass
4. fee—free
5. froj—frog
6. chrain—train
7. prise—prize
8. dive—drive

Math

Sample Test: Concepts 68
1. b
2. a
3. b
4. c

Sample Test: Addition and Subtraction.........................69
3. c
4. b
5. c
6. a
7. c
8. d

Sample Test: Geometry........70
2. b
3. a
4. b
5. a
6. b

Sample Test: Measurement..71
1. b
2. c
3. c
4. a

Small or Large? 72
Square
smallest—3
largest—10

Diamond
smallest—2
largest—9

Circle
smallest—3
largest—20

Rectangle at left
smallest—9
largest—18

Triangle
smallest—9
largest—36

Rectangle at right
smallest—23
largest—42

My Favorite Snacks 73
1. 64   **6.** 96
2. 39   **7.** 98
3. 89   **8.** 78
4. 68   **9.** 78
5. 79

Stepping Out 74
1. 12
2. 23
3. 41
4. 34

Yummy!.................................75
b. fourth
c. twelfth
d. fifteenth
e. tenth
f. sixteenth
g. thirteenth
h. seventh

Picture Fractions 76
Halves—1, 3, 4, 6

How Many Toys? 77

1. 6
2. 9
3. 11
4. 4
5. 6

Farm Life 78

1. 57	9. 75	17. 39
2. 26	10. 68	
3. 91	11. 55	
4. 89	12. 78	
5. 70	13. 33	
6. 89	14. 57	
7. 87	15. 59	
8. 98	16. 59	

Springtime 79

1. 24	10. 22
2. 75	11. 16
3. 60	12. 10
4. 21	13. 51
5. 50	14. 29
6. 33	15. 43
7. 13	16. 31
8. 44	17. 78
9. 4	

Prediction and Probability Beads 80

1. square bead—because it follows the pattern of three round beads, then one square bead
2. round bead—because there are more round beads than square beads

Finding Patterns 81

1. smiley face
2. shamrock
3. circle
4. pen
5. chair
6. cherry

A Summer Picnic 82

1. 3
2. no
3. 3
4. 16

Bouncing Balls....................83

1. 4 balls down and 3 balls across = 12 balls
2. 6 balls down and 4 balls across = 24 balls
3. 5 balls down and 4 balls across = 20 balls
4. 5 balls down and 6 balls across = 30 balls
5. 3 balls down and 4 balls across = 12 balls
6. 3 balls down and 7 balls across = 21 balls

Green Jelly Beans 84

Answers will vary.

A Bear in the Woods 85

1. squirrels
2. rabbits
3. birds
4. squirrels

Ship Shapes........................88

bottom of ship—green
middle of ship—red
windows in middle of ship—yellow
top of ship—orange
water—blue

1. triangle
2. rectangle
3. circle
4. square

The Shape of Things 89

1. color the second shape, R, R, T, T
2. color the third shape, S, R, S
3. color the fourth shape, T, S, R, T

Calculating Caterpillars 91

1. 3, yellow	4. 5, orange
2. 8, red	5. 2, green
3. 4, yellow	6. 6, orange

Helping Out 92

1. 1 quart
2. 8 cups
3. 1 quart
4. 4 pints

It's Time for Vacation!..........93

1. 14 days
2. 2 months
3. 2 months
4. 3 days
5. 1 month
6. quarter of an hour

Space Travel 94

1. 1	9. 1
2. 1	10. 2
3. 1	11. 3
4. 1	12. 2
5. 1	13. 2
6. 1	14. 3
7. 2	15. 1
8. 2	16. 2

rocket 1 — 2 in.
rocket 3 — 8 in.
rocket 9 — 6 in.
rocket 12 — 7 in.
rocket 15 — 3 in.

Weather Watch 95

1. 30°, cold
2. 50°, mild
3. 90°, hot

Time to Go! **96**
1. 8:00 P.M., bath
2. 11:00 A.M., soccer
3. 5:00 P.M., dinner
4. 10:30 A.M., shop
5. 1:00 P.M., read
6. 3:30 P.M., party

Counting Coins **97**
1. 60¢
2. 81¢
3. 67¢

Arctic Animals **98–99**
Graph
polar bear—3
reindeer—1
penguin—6
seal—5

1. 3
2. 1
3. 6
4. 5
5. penguin
6. reindeer
7. 3
8. 4

Science

Sample Test **102**
2. a
3. b
4. a
5. c

Sample Test **103**
2. a
3. b
4. c
5. c

Animal Attributes **104**
1. turtle
2. chicken
3. beaver
4. bird
5. snake
animals that hatch from an
egg—turtle, chicken, bird

Will It Float? **105**
Things that will float—feather,
stick, leaf, egg
Things that will sink—rock, nail,
spoon, paper

What Are Clouds? **106**
Starting in bottom right corner—
picture of water evaporating
into air (b); picture of clouds
absorbing moisture (c); picture
of dark clouds with rain coming
down from them (a)

All Types of Matter **107**
1. X—umbrella, liquids
2. X—sea or ocean, gases
3. X—pitcher of water, solids

Animal Kingdom **108**
1. penguin, sea
2. cow, land
3. pig, land
4. bee, air
5. bird, air
6. fish, sea

Animal Babies **109**
1. d, piglet
2. a, lamb
3. b, duckling
4. c, kitten

Social Studies

Sample Test **112**
2. c
3. b
4. a

Sample Test **113**
2. a
3. b
4. a

In America,
We Are Free To **114**
1. a
2. d
3. c
4. b

Our Constitution **115**
Scrolls to color—Washington,
D.C., rights, 200 years ago,
freedoms, laws

Money Earned **116**
First Store—26¢, apple
Second Store—82¢, yo-yo
Third Store—40¢, greeting card
Fourth Store—$1.00, sundae
Fifth Store—57¢, fish

What Is a Globe? **117**
1. no
2. yes
3. yes
4. no
5. no
6. yes
7. yes
8. no

Asking Directions **118**
1. north
2. east
3. south
4. west

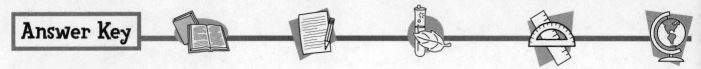
Thomas Edison 119
1. d
2. c
3. a
4. b

Where Do You Live? 120
1. b
2. c
3. d
4. a

Finding Friends on the Map 121–122
1. California (blue)
2. Arizona (red)
3. Colorado (green)
4. Utah (purple)
5. Nevada, New Mexico, Oklahoma, Texas, and Wyoming (yellow)
6. **a.** California beach
   b. Nuru
7. **a.** Utah
   b. Hanni
8. **a.** Arizona
   b. Max
9. **a.** Colorado
   b. Aleka